MIGRANT JOURNEY

MIGRANT JOURNEY

Olga Russo Waters

For my children and my grandchildren

Foreword

We never forget the child we once were

For her, it is a page of her history and the fulfillment of a dream. For us, it is an example and a tribute to all of those people who have known and still know exile today or have been driven out by misery, poverty or cruelty.

Within and around this story is an abundance of humanity intertwined with the modesty of Olga Russo. There is also a suffering of uprooting as experienced by North Africans, Polish and Italians who settled in the Nord of France who, in turn, needed laborers in their mines after World War II.

Likewise, there is a richness of emotion and tenderness of a childhood at the heart of a family shattered and wounded by the vagaries of life. There is the love and admiration of a little girl for her father that she will cherish forever. There is affection of a child for her school girlfriends from whom she was abruptly separated and whose ineffable memory is etched in her heart.

There is also immense pride to find, even a half century later, traces of the simple and beautiful years she had lived before a departure to the "Eldorado" of the New World. There is the courage and determination of an admirable and supportive family that has been able to give meaning to its life without ever, even for a moment, forgetting the "Nord" that had marked and illuminated a childhood.

Finally, there are brief but intense moments of youth nourished by a flame of love that has never been extinguished over the generations which has been revived thanks to this story.

I could not have imagined that my book *Memoirs of a Child of the Nord* could have reached across nine thousand kilometers from "my native Nord" to reactivate the embers of the early childhood in Olga's heart that she secretly preserved in a universe of memories that, in fact, never left her. A true and moving story, a moment of sharing, a model of courage and success, a lesson in life!

Jacques Pagniez

TABLE OF CONTENTS

1

My birthplace in Italy

Once upon a time...far away and into the countryside of the Puglia region of Southern Italy, cradled at the foot of Mount San Marco was *Orsara di Puglia*, my native land. That quaint little village with its houses all crowded in its center, surrounded by miles and miles of wheat fields, vineyards and olive groves, formed a striking panorama on the mountainside. Its population fluctuated between two and three thousand villagers over the course of time.

Similar picturesque villages dotted the six provinces that made up the region of Puglia. The region was bordered by the Adriatic Sea on the east, the Ionic Sea on the southeast, and the Strait of Otranto and Gulf of Taranto on the south. A limestone plateau and the Itria Valley formed the central part of the region. The Gargano, the spur of the boot, constituted one of the most breathtaking sceneries of my life. Its mountainous area filled with beech, birch, yew and pine trees was part of the Umbra Forest, the only portion of the ancient Black Forest that remained in Italy. The coast of the Gargano was rich in beaches and more charming little villages with stories of their own.

Our region was well-known for producing strong wines that were frequently used to fortify other lighter varieties. As a little girl with a sweet tooth, the best part of winemaking was the aroma of our cooked wine filling the air. It was an exquisite syrup that had simmered for nearly eighteen hours to reach its perfect consistency. We used it to flavor desserts or, sometimes, we discretely stole a sip from the bottle. For my deep love for salt, I felt obliged to share that it was produced from the seawater at Margherita di Savoia near *Foggia*, the capital of our province. *Foggia* was also the closest big city situated at a distance of roughly twenty-five miles from *Orsara*.

Our village had officially become part of the Puglia Region in 1927. Several legends existed on how the name of *Orsara* evolved from its Latin name

Castrum Ursariae. My personal favorite was one of the many stories my paternal nonno[1] charmed me with when I met him at the age of nine. *Castrum* meant a fortified site, *ursa,* a female bear and *ariae* an open space. Hence, *Orsara* was a fortified place where bears once lived. For our "real story"... *In ancient times, the Greek hero Diomedes returned home to Greece after battle. Distraught over his wife's infidelity, he departed Greece and ventured into Southern Italy. As battles ensued, he was compelled to set up a camp where his wounded soldiers could heal. They settled in the middle of a huge forest full of caves where Diomedes built a fortified camp atop of one of those caves which was home to a mama bear and her two cubs.*

Life in *Orsara* evolved over time, but the town proper remained relatively unchanged. For nearly two decades, *Orsara* was the only face of Italy known to me. A charming village with a very hard life. My little village fashioned from the 1950s to 1970s, was liberally brought to life by the memory of my young years, a handful of photos, family visits over the years and through countless stories told by my family and their friends. Many of which, surely should not have been eavesdropped on, but my curiosity...was my curiosity.

Orsara was an outdoor town. It gave the impression of entering into the past and stepping back in time to share in the life of our ancestors. The square cobblestone pavers on the streets were traversed from dawn until well past dusk by busy people and workers who came and went on their long journey to their fields, mostly on foot. Their mules were loaded with their tools and their crops.

The residential portion of the village was compact. It took only an hour to walk from one end to the other, however, two hours were necessary to chat with friends along the way. Throughout the day, women balanced barrels of water or baskets full of laundry on their heads to and from the fountain. The young children played on the pavers here and there while the older ones were in the fields alongside their parents.

Its roads were steep and narrow. Some were so abrupt, intermittent steps softened their incline. Most roads resembled narrow pathways with tiny platforms which provided entry to homes that had been passed down from generation to generation. The dwellings were modest, typically composed of one or two rooms. The indoor space included a stall for their mule or horse if they were lucky enough to own one. Families who owned a pig, placed them in a small open niche around the chimney, always close to the front door where they were able to keep an eye on it. In the fall, the pig was butchered and its meat was dried for consumption over the following year.

---

[1] Nonno: Grandfather in Italian; nonni (plural).

The inhabitants were mostly poor and lived an agricultural life. Their production during that time was still exclusively manual and reserved for the family's personal consumption. They sold or exchanged a portion of their harvest for commodities they needed or could not produce themselves. Similar to most families during that time, mine toiled for long days throughout the year in several fields scattered on the outskirts of the village. Some took two or three hours to reach by foot and were sometimes in diametrically opposing directions. Occasionally, people swapped comparable parcels of land to reduce that problem. The areas where the fields were situated had been named by the villagers of past generations primarily for a point of reference and to easily find one another.

Although Italian had become the formal language after the Kingdom of Italy formed in 1860, like each of their neighboring villages who spoke their own dialect, ours spoke *Orsaresi* Formal Italian was taught in school. Since my paternal great-grandfather had come from the big city of Naples, my grandfather grew up speaking proper Italian. His ancestors in Naples had been tax collectors for the King. The abolishment of the kingdom eliminated those types of jobs, forcing entire families to move elsewhere, anywhere they were able to find work. My great-grandfather, a widower, and his three young children moved in the village of *Orsara*. There, he married another widow. Together they had two other children, Nonno Alfredo and Pasquale.

The village was in essence its own tiny little world. It was run by a mayor elected by its residents. All basic civil functions were managed within the village. Our police dealt with public order and ensured that businesses opened and closed in accordance with their license. During the time when my parents were young, there was a prison in the middle of the village. Surrounding the building, a thick stone wall was topped with shards of glass to prevent prisoners from escaping as the other side almost rubbed shoulders with the houses. My mom's childhood home stood directly behind the prison. When their window was open on nice days, routine conversations held in the courtyard by prisoners were easily overheard.

A great richness of our village was its history and its architecture. It was adorned with Byzantine, Baroque and Romanesque styles that had influenced the Puglia region over many centuries. In the oldest part of the village, remnants of a medieval wall that was formerly reinforced with square towers that were once armed to protect the village, were still visible. Over time, when the wall was no longer necessary for protection, *Orsara* opened up its doors to their nearby villages that had been destroyed. As *Orsara* grew, parts of its medieval enclosure were absorbed by the new dwellings. Surrounding the village were three canals that had formed a moat-like natural defense in ancient times to protect them against their frequent invaders.

The heart of the village was the *Saint Michele* complex. It consisted of two ancient churches connected by a cave, the *Grotta of Saint Michele, the Archangel*. The cave was partly natural and partly carved by hand. It was believed to be a stopover on the pilgrimage route to one of the oldest shrines in Western Europe devoted to *Saint Michele*, the Gargano *Sanctuary of Mount Saint Angelo.* Nearby was *Giovanni Rodondo,* home to Padre Pio of *Pietrelcina* from 1916 until 1968.

The *Grotta* adjoined the *Saint Pellegrino* church built in the 17th Century that according to legends owed its name to a visit by San Pellegrino, and the *Annunziata* church which was built around the 10th or 11th Century. The *Annunziata* church was constructed with an internal wall which formed a tunnel. According to tales, that passageway, once secret, was used as an escape route to discreetly and rapidly allow people to flee from the village in times of turmoil. Around 1600, the parish moved to the church of *Saint Nicola di Bari* situated in the center of the village. That beautiful construction built around the late 11th Century was my family's place of worship.

At a few paces from the church, stood a stone archway that led into the courtyard of the *Saint Angelo Abbey*. The monastery, built around the 12th Century, had once been equipped with chambers to accommodate the pilgrims on their way to the Gargano. After multiple sales over the centuries, a feudal family with the surname of Guevara purchased it. They subsequently renamed it the *Palace of the Barons* as it is still known today. During the Guevara ownership, they added a balcony overlooking the church which allowed the noble family direct access to their place of worship from their home.

Around 1900, a part of that building was used as a school. It was at the *Palace of the Barons* that my own parents attended elementary school. The boys took the staircase on the right of the building while the girls took the one on the left. By then, that structure was so cold and dilapidated that it was difficult to ever imagine it as a palace, or to dream of fairytales. During the winter months, the children each brought their own tin container filled with some smoldering coal, which they placed under their bench for a bit of warmth throughout their day.

During that period, a fifth grade education was obligatory in *Orsara*. An exemption could be granted as early as the third grade to families in cases of hardship so the children could work alongside their parents. Few children had the means to commute into the large city of *Foggia* every day for an education beyond the fifth grade.

While electricity had illuminated the homes of our village in 1925, other improvements of comfort were non-nonexistent. As late as the 1950s, the dwellings in the village still did not have running water. Water for all of its inhabitants came from one of several fountains in the periphery. The "new" fountain built in the 1400s was situated on the *Palace of the Barons'* complex for obvious reasons. Two beautiful large stone arches led to the main tub. Women knelt on the hard stone to do their laundry in the troughs situated at the base of the right and the left wall. Like everything else, it too was another grueling chore, especially for heavily stained items that needed to be bleached. First, it was washed at the canal or the fountain with the rest of the laundry, then it was brought home un-rinsed. After treating the stains with bleach, the items were piled into a large metal container. A clean cloth, lined with ashes that were scraped from the fireplace, was draped over the top. Boiling water from the cauldron was poured over the ashes and through the cloth until it filled the container. The laundry soaked overnight. In the morning, the plug underneath was released to allow the water to drain. To rinse, the women transported the wash back to the fountain on their heads by foot or by mule.

Water for human consumption in the village predominantly came from the *Saint Angelo* fountain on one extreme of the main road, *Corso della Vittoria.* The "*Corso,*" was the longest and widest road that ran from one end of the village to the other. That fountain's location along with its spherical structure that accommodated water spouts all around it, made the area a primary site for congregation. There, women filled their wooden barrels with water which they carried home on their heads. To soften the hardness of the wood and to stabilize the barrel, an old rag twisted in a circular fashion was placed between their head and the barrel. At home, they transferred the water into glass jugs or a sealed cement tub. Alongside the fountain was also a massive trough with running water that offered mules and horses the opportunity to quench their thirst after a long hard day in the fields.

On the other end of the "*Corso*" was a tiny woodland known as the Pine Forest. It was occupied by pine trees on one hillside and chestnut trees on the other. As this place was reputed for the purity of its air, it had become "the place" of remedy by the village doctor for those who suffered with a respiratory problem or another ailment that had no label at the time. There, the sick inhaled the pure air, the young children played and women picked dandelions. From early morning until late evening, people swarmed this haven. I was amazed to learn, years later, that the land was not public property. Ostensibly, the entire world was there and no one was ever asked to leave. The Pine Forest and its lovely cottage on the hilltop belonged to the very wealthy family by the surname of Maffei. By the 1950s, the cottage that had once been full of workers and animals was occupied by only a handful of people tending to the property.

5

The Maffei family employed many *Orsaresi* to work in their plethora of businesses and land that they owned all around the village. Even my paternal great-grandparents were fortunate to have worked all together, as a family, on one of their countless farms tending to their animals. Other villagers, including my maternal nonni, rented land to supplement the shortcomings of their own fields. The land my grandparents had rented was difficult to cultivate, in part, because it had a stream running through it. What had proved most valuable to my grandparents on that property, was the out-of-service mill that sheltered their animals during the winter months. As for the stream, my grandfather, Nonno Paolo, used it to create an irrigation system. First he dug small canals throughout the property, then filled them with rocks that he had cleared from other parts of the property to make it tillable. Since that land required an abundance of work, it was not particularly useful to its proprietor. Mom always said that their payment was miniscule. It amounted to two small mounds of their fava bean harvest.

The wealthy entrepreneurs lived in a massive building, equating to a New York City block, in the center of the village. A gigantic warehouse made up part of the structure. From time to time, Mom sent my sister, Elisa, to buy various goods. For all of her chores, coming to the Maffei warehouse was her favorite. In awe, she gazed at a countless selection of olive oil, cheese and an abundance of other items that she could not name. She always wished for her order to be delayed to immerse in all of the gastronomic riches on the fully stocked shelves that made her dream a little longer. There were other shops in the village, but this was the only establishment where one could buy in bulk and more easily exchange goods for cash.

A variety of smaller shops including tailors, butchers, cafés, bars and the town ovens were sprinkled throughout the village. For a stranger, it was not easy to discern most businesses from homes, they all blended together. Businesses were typically part of a two-room house. The shop occupied the front room with the dwelling in the other. Signs to identify the shops were pointless because everyone knew one another. Moreover, everyone always knew where to go for what. Plaques were merely an essence of pride.

Among the handful of tailors in town, Gilda was, by far, the most luxurious with its large glass display windows. The interior was equally impressive with walls stacked from floor to ceiling illuminated by an array of fabrics. It was also the most expensive, making it unaffordable for my family. Most clothing, including undergarments, were handmade by either a tailor or a seamstress. A variety of fabric was available but, by and large, the most durable was chosen.

In our time, shops with ready-made shoes or clothing were nonexistent in our village. No doubt, this explained my love for shoes in my later years. Lots of shoes! Shoemakers custom made our shoes and repaired them when necessary. Similar to many *Orsaresi,* my grandfathers were adept in making minor repairs.

Ready-made clothes could only be bought at the open market. The most popular was directly behind the *Saint Angelo* fountain under a huge sheltered space owned by the Mastropiere family whose dwelling sat conveniently above it. On the street level, two stone arches gave way into a protected area that was leased to vendors from nearby villages to spread their goods. It was a prime location to shield vendors from the harsh weather as they slept on the ground near their belongings at night. One of the regular vendors from Naples sold colorful "American" dresses in the style of the time. Mom once bought a seven layer dress in its largest size for the extra fabric. After disassembling it, she sewed new clothes for all of us. Major holidays attracted additional vendors who sold shoes, trousers, china and various other gadgets that could typically only be purchased in bigger villages like *Troia* or in the large city of *Foggia.*

Small consumable products such as salt, paper, stamps and envelopes were sold in a general store or a *Tabacchi* which was a smaller general store authorized to sell tobacco. Salt pieces were preserved in large sacs. Each piece sold was prudently weighed at the counter. For the coarser pieces, they were easily smashed at home using a wooden block.

A few bars and cafés were scattered around the village. The one located nearest to us by the *Saint Angelo* fountain was the only two-level establishment. The café on the main level served cookies, ice cream and coffee. In the bar downstairs, the men congregated to play cards, discuss politics or other matters of the world. Children were never permitted downstairs and women in any bar were frowned upon.

My father occasionally met buddies at the bar for a beer or a card game of Scopa or Briscola. If he lost track of time, Mom sent Elisa up the street to summon him. Even at five years old, she was bold, spunky and far beyond her years. She took all of her responsibilities seriously, including her mission to retrieve her father for dinner. Knowing the bar was forbidden to her, she discreetly passed through the café. As she neared the stairs, she ran quickly to avoid being caught by the owner, Pasquale, who howled as he pretended to chase her. The faster she ran, the harder Pasquale laughed. She delivered the message to her father that dinner was ready, but she did not budge until he physically stood up. Mom must have warned her not to leave without him. On the way back, as she approached the top of the staircase, she ran past Pasquale who was already waiting for her and pretended to chase her out of the bar until the next time.

In our butcher shops, we bought meat and sold or traded livestock. Raising livestock did not necessarily mean one ate meat. My maternal nonna[2] raised sheep, pigs, and goats. When the family needed cash for things they could not grow or make themselves, she sold one of the animals from her farm.

Bakeries in our village were nonexistent and most inhabitants had no means to bake at home since most stoves were not equipped with ovens. Instead, we had village ovens that largely baked bread. Their system was efficient and simple. On our pre-arranged day, a single knock on the door signaled the time to begin mixing the dough. We grew our own wheat and bought our yeast. Oftentimes, yeast starter was shared with neighbors who needed it.

The baker delivered three foot long wooden planks at our door. The large loaves were placed those planks where they began to rise, then the planks were picked up at a designated time and transported to the village oven. There, after the dough finished rising, it was baked in their straw fueled oven. Although the baker always knew who to return each loaf of bread to, each family uniquely marked theirs. Mom's was a simple thin pencil-like roll of dough across the top of the loaf, lightly pinched on each end. Payment, like everything else, was cash or goods plus a baker's loaf which was a smaller loaf of bread destined for the baker's personal consumption or to sell to those who could afford to buy it. Town ovens stayed open every single day of the year with Sundays and holidays as their busiest days.

Most holiday celebrations in our village were associated with a saint and a procession that began or ended at the *Grotta* cave. The nuns typically organized the children's participation in the processions for the holy days. As a young boy, even my father took part in those ceremonies. On the sacred days, the children paraded through the streets together. At stops designated by the nuns, various children took their stage on a dweller's balcony for a biblical recitation in front of all the proud parents bordering the streets on their route. There were two groups of nuns in *Orsara* during that time period. They were simply named by the color of their habits, the "black sisters" lived in the *San Domenico Convent* and the "white sisters" lived in the *Varo Palace.*[3]

The *Varo Palace* had been acquired by the Diocese of Troy in the early 1900s to convert into a convent and boarding school for the sisters in white who came from many different parts of the country. Although their exposure to the northern and western lifestyle gave them a more worldly wise view, other than teaching Sunday catechism or organizing the children's participation in

---

[2] Nonna: Grandmother in Italian; nonni (plural).
[3] *Varo Palace*: Built in the 16th century by the noble family Varo.

8

the processions, they did not interact with the general community. A sighting of a sister in white, other than on the holy days, was rare.

One exception was around the Christmas holidays. It was the only time of the year that the gigantic doors of the palace remained open to the public. Their magnificent exhibition of the Town of Bethlehem, the city of nativity that spread over several rooms had, without a doubt, taken months of effort to create. Their meticulous production, all predominantly crafted with natural products that they had collected in and around the village, was stunning. A huge skylight in the center of the palace opened onto the skies overhead, illuminating their spectacle with its bright sparkling stars that along with their elegant and complex lighting throughout, even made their snow look real. The moss used to cover the rooftops had come from a particular area of the woods on the outskirts of the village. It left everyone in awe as they pondered when they had collected those items since they were rarely seen in the community. My parents, akin to countless other villagers, returned to see this splendor over and over again. On that rare occasion, the nuns took their time to explain all of the particulars about the materials used to create the masterpiece and the significance of their display to all of their visitors.

The convent for the sisters in black was situated in the *Saint Domenico Complex* which was built around 1600. In addition to teaching catechism and organizing the children's involvement in processions, they taught elementary school and skills such as embroidery to young girls and adults. Directly behind the church, a fence surrounded a huge playground. Each Sunday afternoon, the sisters unlocked the gate, granting permission to the young children of all denominations, already lined up, to enter and play.

While most holidays celebrated in our village were religious, by far, the biggest celebration was that of *Saint Michele, the Archangel*. It was so significant that the *Orsaresi* celebrated it twice. The official celebration occurred on September 29. A lesser ado instituted by Pope Pius V (1566-1572) was celebrated on May 8. It commemorated the apparition of the *Archangel* in *Mount Gargano* which took place not too far away.

The extraordinary *Fucacoste* was a massive chain of bonfires lit for *All Saints Day*, November 1. It was thought that on that day, the souls returned home to reunite with the spirit of their loved ones before moving on to paradise. With the toll of the church bells at dusk, all of the bonfires throughout the streets were ignited simultaneously, burning all through the night. The glow in the streets helped each of the souls to find their way home.

A traditional dish prepared for that day was *Muscitaglia*, a boiled grain dish believed to date back to ancient times. The grain soaked overnight. After adding a pinch of salt, it simmered for several hours. When the grain expanded and burst, it was drained and drizzled with some cooked wine. In the evening, potatoes, sausages and chestnuts cooked on the burning embers in the streets were shared with family and friends.

Two other much-loved patrons in our village were *Saint Anthony* and *Saint Rocco*. The patron saint of fire and healer of the plague, *Saint Anthony* was celebrated in mid-January. It was customary for mothers to dress their young children in the *Saint Anthony* habit on that day. My mom carried the tradition to France with the birth of my little brothers. She sewed the long sleeve black tunic that fell just above the knees. A wide black collar overlaid a slimmer white collar and a white cord was tied around the waistline. The chain holding a Saint Anthony charm and the tunic were taken to church for the blessing, then my brothers wore the outfit for the rest of the day.

Saint Rocco, another healer of the plague, was celebrated in August. Many *Orsaresi* who had settled in eastern Pennsylvania often met fellow Italians at the Saint Rocco Festival held in Roseto, Pennsylvania. One of the fondest recollections of my youth was on our first visit to the festival in 1968. While my father drove us through high festive traffic, an abrupt burst of swearing spilled from his lips. It was focused on a group of people frozen in place in the middle of the street, facing our car. Upon coming face to face with our driver, the strangers became equally animated. Interpreting the blubbering sounds was confusing. That crowd was not familiar to me, but the situation quickly became apparent. The adults immediately abandoned our car while the children observed long embraces and joyful tears among them. There, in the middle of the street stood *Orsaresi* friends of my parents, the once owners of a village oven. Both of our families had emigrated from *Orsara* around the same time with the hope of finding a better life. Their destination had been Argentina while ours was France. Our two families had immigrated at a different time to two separate destinations. By happenstance, more than a decade later, the friends met again on a third continent!

Through countless conversations and exchanges over the years, the shortcomings of our charming little village in Southern Italy became clearer. My father often said, "You can't eat scenery." In desperation, people had left their homes and their families. Their destinations were different whereas their motives were all too similar. Despite the renewals brought forth by the twentieth century and the global upheaval with industrialization in the northern part of Italy, the south lagged behind. Our village had not benefited from those transformations in time for many of us.

Villagers worked hard to simply survive. With no prospect of improving day-to-day life, many were forced to look elsewhere. The lacking economy in Southern Italy made it a reservoir for labor after WWII. With little or no experience necessary, people were willing to take on any means of labor as long as they had a guaranteed income. My family was no different. We too began to disperse. Siblings of both my maternal and paternal grandparents immigrated to the United States of America. From there, when they could, they called for one another to join them.

To address some of the problems, various subsidies had been established in Southern Italy for agriculture and to build an infrastructure for housing, roads, schools and hospitals that was inadequate and insufficient. Unfortunately, the criteria and distribution for the allocation of agricultural subsidies was sometimes ambiguous. Oftentimes, the allocations were ineffective because many still lacked the necessary equipment or the knowledge to operate them. Their land was still cultivated by archaic and inefficient methods. As for employment in building an infrastructure, the problems were similar. Jobs with a steady pay were difficult to acquire and many lacked the skills necessary to fill those positions.

It forced many to remain in the fields where, much like the first half of the century in our village, reaping, threshing and winnowing was still done by hand, primarily on site, in the fields. The mules transported heavy loads of wheat stalks up to the threshing area. The highest point of elevation on their land was used to benefit from the highest winds. Once there, the mules knew what to do. They crushed the stalks and loosened the grain by pulling a crushing stone in circles over the threshing area. My maternal Nonno Paolo dug a large flat limestone from the canal that ran through his field. The stone was soft enough for him to pierce holes in it and thread a rope through it. Mom told me that she and her younger siblings took turns sitting atop of the stone for the added weight while their mule pulled them around and around the threshing area.

Mules were invaluable. Their loss was catastrophic as my mom discovered very young. Mules were terrified of steps and, more often than not, stalls were inside the houses. Because my grandparents had a stairway leading to their front door, they were forced to rent a house nearby to keep theirs. He was rarely left alone and someone always spent nights with him. On one of those few times that the mule was left unattended, it was stolen. Without that indispensable aide at the onset of wheat harvest, it was disastrous. That essential assistance was needed to transport, to seed, to pull the plow and to get to hard-to-reach terrain. Without the mule, harvesting was impossible. Without harvesting, the family starved.

My grandparents had no choice but to purchase another mule. The problem was cash, or lack thereof. They came to an accord with the vendor to pay half in cash, the rest would be in exchange for labor in the sellers' fields. For 3,000 Liras[4] plus six years of labor, my grandparents purchased a new mule. As a

---

[4] 3000 Liras: Approximately $4,630 in current day money.

result, my mother gave up starting her fifth grade. She was removed from school to work alongside her older sister, Felice. Working together, the debt was paid in three years instead of six but Mom continued to work in the fields until she married my father.

Other difficulties prevalent around that time were diseases. Within the generation of my parents, most aunts and uncles lost several young children. The church bell tolled with each death of fellow villagers. Their smaller bell was reserved for the young lives lost. There was no mistaking the tolling of the small bell that was heard every single day for a very long time. The cause of death was often unknown. Grief and despair, on the other hand, were known far too well.

Over time, the conditions of daily life had not improved much. Many people, left with no other alternative, continued to disperse throughout the world. When nothing was left, why not try someplace else? Siblings of my grandparents on both sides left for America before I was born. Some aunts and uncles migrated with their families to Northern Italy where they worked in the factories. By word of mouth and seeing money that arrived home to the families left behind, the news about the abundance of work in other places spread. The idea of working in a job with a stable wage was attractive. Villagers read extraordinary stories about different lifestyles in letters from their loved ones urging them to join those departed. So, relatives called for one another to hope and opportunity. Relatives who could, joined others already gone...and so on...and so on...

Leaving misery behind also meant leaving family and a familiar place to move toward a life paved with uncertainty. Many villagers, including my own relatives, scattered around different parts of the world hoping they too could earn enough money to return home after a few years to buy a house and a bit of land to live a more comfortable and normal life. It was also my father's plan. Then, life happened. Like many other families with stories of their own, our world was turned upside down and changed forever.

2

My little family

Clip-clop, clip-clop, clip-clop…Horseshoes rapped against the cobblestones and harnesses jangled. It was five o'clock in morning, the time when villagers, mules and horses left their homes to go to work in their fields. On an ordinary workday, my mom and my paternal great-grandmother, Mamma Antonia, joined the convoy to the fields.

On that particular day, they stayed home because my father, affectionately called Pop, had just returned from his military service. He had journeyed overnight by train from *Pinerolo* where he had served as a Sergeant Major in a cavalry regiment of the Alpine Brigade of Turin. As it was a period of peace in Italy, the obligatory eighteen months of service for his "Class of 1927" had not been particularly stressful except for the separation from his family. While in the service, he was part of a mountain artillery group that trained with a light infantry brigade of the Italian army specializing in mountain combat on horses. He had become one of their best jumpers. His only permission home had been six months earlier when Elisa was born in June 1949.

With almost nothing to unpack from his satchel, Pop easily found the gifts he had brought for his little princess. Eyes sparkling and a smile from ear to ear, he pulled out two adorable dresses. One was pink and the other was light blue, his favorite color. White shoes and knee socks completed the ensemble.

Pop was a charismatic young man. My mother was beautiful and soft-spoken. Both were just over five feet tall, thin, had chestnut hair and dark brown eyes. They complemented one another beautifully. Dance gatherings had brought them together in their teens. On Sundays, when they were not hard at work in the fields, they saw one another among friends. Pop played mandolin, his friends accompanied on violin and guitar. Their dance floor had effortlessly materialized in the house as the teenagers pushed beds, table and chairs against the wall. Even then, my mother had known she loved Pop and covertly treasured the moments that her own father had chased her Romeo away while serenading under their window.

Mamma Antonia, who adored my parents, had invited them to live with her after they eloped. Mamma was always by Mom's side. She was a tiny, hardworking, high spirited and well-loved seventy year old woman. After Elisa was born, my mother's work in the field was limited so she and Mamma Antonia were exclusively responsible for guarding the vineyard, a far less arduous job. Together, with baby Elisa, they spent their nights in a small straw hut. During the day while Elisa napped, Mom weeded or pinched back the grapes. On laundry day, villagers dropped off her mother-in-law's laundry on the way to their own fields. Mom washed it all in the canal nearby, then hung it up to dry. The laundry was collected by the villagers when they passed by for their return trip home in the evening.

Labor in the vineyard typically ended with the grape harvest. The wine was made on site in the fields. It was one of the most festive gatherings for our family. My paternal grandparents had a gigantic wooden container that they assembled on the grounds of the orchard once per year to make the wine. Stomping the grapes was the most amusing part. All feet touching the grapes were meticulously washed. Women had a free pass to show more of their legs because their dresses needed to be pulled up above the knees.

The enormous tub held up by large sturdy wooden legs stood approximately three feet off the ground, leaving enough space to insert multiple large containers to catch the juice that poured from the small holes beneath it. The grape juice was then transferred into small barrels that the mules hauled back to the village, three barrels at a time. They carried one on each side with a third on its back. At home, the small barrels filled the much larger oak barrels in our cave that, within a few months, transformed the juice into wine. A small portion was destined for the delicious slow-cooked wine.

Stomping the grapes did not fully squeeze out all of the juice and, again, nothing was wasted. That residue of pits, skins and other particles was prudently recovered. After distillation in the purity of the night in our house, that precious material gave us an excellent spirit whose medicinal virtues that had been praised by our ancestors are still recognized today.

Our house was located near the *Saint Angelo* fountain. The cobblestone road that led to our street, *Via Tasso,* was so steep that a shallow step spaced at every few yards was needed to ease the slope. Our street always reminded me of a terrace overhanging on the side of a mountain. It was short, wide and bordered on each side by roughly six row houses. On one end of our street, a narrow staircase descended onto a side road. On the other extreme, another very steep alleyway sprinkled with steps softened its descent to a secondary road below us and a climb to the *"Corso"* above us. Another row of dwellings sat on our rooftops whose entrances were on the street above and behind ours.

Via Tasso #7 was a modest one-room dwelling. Our front door opened to tall white plaster walls curving into a vaulted ceiling. Dried sausages and prosciutto hung from hooks to keep them safe from rodents. Pop devoted one of his first paychecks to cover our uneven brick floor with cement. Thin lines painted in green gave it the appearance of a warm ceramic tiled floor. One wall was decorated with Pop's mandolin, the others with an assortment of dried peppers and braided garlic.

A wood burning fireplace that heated our home stood against the wall beside the entrance. A triangular device supporting the inside of the fireplace also served to hang a large cauldron alongside other pots to boil water. Beside it, a small built-in stovetop that was connected to the chimney duct was routinely used for cooking. The ever-present coffee pot sitting on one of the two burner portable electric stove was always ready to receive guests. For our colder days, a wooden circular portable heater with a metal basin was placed in the center of the room for some extra heat. The fireplace, stove and portable heater were all fueled by charcoal made from dry branches in our fields that had been burned and then crushed into shavings.

Our home was simply furnished. The toilette corner alongside the front door consisted of a tiny wooden table holding a shallow white ceramic basin. Its center drawer hid our toiletries and a small cloth hung on one side. Nearby were the glass jugs filled with fresh water that were always on hand for drinking, cooking and other necessities. Our furniture was all handmade with the walnut trees that grew in my maternal nonno's fields. It was customary in our village that for newly married couples, the males provided the "roof" while the women furnished it. Depending on what families were able to afford, some couples started their life together with more, some with less. Mom's parents did not have money, but their land was rich in walnut trees.

Our huge table surrounded by six chairs commanded the center of the room. Beside the electric stove, another gorgeous walnut cabinet stored flour. Its cover doubled as a kneading board when it was flipped. My mother used it to mix dough for bread and pasta several times per week. On the opposite wall, a tall wooden grain bin that was divided into several vertical compartments stored the wheat, corn, beans and oats that we had harvested. A small hatch at the bottom dispensed our necessities. As needed, we took small amounts of grain to the general store to be ground into flour. A small portion of the grain was always held in reserve for the following year's seeding. Before sowing,

15

that grain was treated with bluestone to prevent the growth of fungus that oftentimes infested the plants.

The matrimonial bed and an armoire draped with lanky mirrors resting against the back wall, demarcated that space as the bedroom. On special occasions, a beautiful rose satin bedspread, a wedding gift from Mom's parents, decorated their bed. Wedged in a small corner nearby was Elisa's cot who split her nights with the one on the loft with Mamma Antonia while she was still with us. The loft, accessible by a wooden ladder leaning against the back wall, pooled as a small bedroom and storage for potatoes, apples or anything that did not fit anywhere else.

Thanks to my maternal grandparents, our mattresses were stuffed with pure sheep wool which made them more comfortable and warmer in the winter. Despite their somewhat irregular shape, my mother had a knack to give the mattresses a flawlessly flat surface. This talent had earned her an award to make the bed at her mother in law's home each morning.

The king of our little castle was Mr. Baron. He stayed in his stall directly beneath the loft when he was not hard at work in the fields. Like most mules, he feared steps so we hid the narrow step in our entryway by covering it with a large burlap sack. We positioned old rags all along his path to the stall at the other end of the house to avoid dung droppings on the floor. Since Mr. Baron worked the hardest, he was served his breakfast and dinner in the largest wooden bowl that we possessed. His mid-day meal was stuffed in a burlap sack and taken to the field where he ate when everyone stopped for a lunch break. Mr. Baron ate like an ogre! He especially loved oats which we grew specifically for him.

Given his close proximity to the spousal bed, his stall was kept virtually spotless. Early each morning, a man we called Michelangelo sounded a trumpet as he neared each neighborhood with his donkey pulled metal sewage tank. When the bright, piercing sound reached ours, we lined up along with our neighbors to empty our waste, human and animal, into a funnel-like opening of the reservoir on the rear of the chamber.

A few steps on the far side of the stall descended into our own natural rock cave that was big enough for a family of bears. Large oak barrels wedged on platforms on one side of the cave cooked the wine. Nearby, the glass demijohns dressed in braided wicker were on standby to store wine for our everyday consumption. On the opposite wall, the terra cotta and aluminum containers filled with olives, honey and peppers, shared their space with other cured meats that hung from the ceiling.

All of our grandparents lived nearby. In Italy, we called them "nonni." Our grandmothers were called "nonna" and our grandfathers, "nonno." With the exception of my paternal nonno, all of my ancestors originated from *Orsara* and were all born around 1900. No one ever forgot to celebrate my Nonno Alfredo's birthday. He was born on January 1, 1900, the first day of the twentieth century! As work in the field was not compatible with school hours, Nonno Alfredo was my only grandparent who had received an education higher than the fifth grade. He had pursued several years of intermediary education through a mail correspondence program. My maternal grandparents were not as fortunate. Family obligations precluded them both from going to school at all as they began to work even younger than most other children.

The home of my paternal Nonni Alfredo and Leonarda was a five minute walk down the street on *Via della Madonna Neve*. Nonna Leonarda was a strong and clever woman. Her older brother had immigrated to California in his teens and never returned. When her father died at a very young age, she inherited all of the family property. A rarity for women of that time. She had never worked in the fields. When children and grand-children arrived, she cared for them during the day which unconstrained the older children as well as other family members to work in the fields. Nonna was well-known for not depriving herself of life's pleasures. It was not uncommon for her to leave the children in the care of others as she covertly escaped by bus to enjoy the beaches or other excursions outside of the village. Now and then, she secretly sold some of the family grain to pay for her outings. Never too much at a time so as not to attract attention.

Nonno Alfredo was very proud and kindhearted with a very charming personality. He was an ardent worker, good-humored and always cheerful. Nonno was irresistible with all of his little stories that he adored sharing with whoever listened. A quality that Pop proudly inherited. Three of Nonno's older siblings, Anzelmo, Emilia and Antimo, had immigrated to the United States of America around the 1940s.

My paternal nonni had four children: Concetta, Giovanna, Michelino (Pop) and Antimo. The small bell in the village tolled for three other children who died very young of various illnesses that were unknown or had no treatments during that time. The eldest, Concetta, and Pop worked together alongside Nonno Alfredo in the fields since their young age of twelve. Pop, like his father, had the good fortune to complete two years beyond his fifth grade education through a mail correspondence program. As the work in the field became more arduous, Pop was forced to abandon further education. He worked in the fields until he left for his military service. Pop's youngest brother, Antimo, found employment as a mechanic's apprentice in *Foggia* after he completed his elementary education.

The land in which Nonno Alfredo worked included a parcel allotted for his military service, the land Nonna Leonarda had inherited from her father, as well as a parcel of land bequeathed to Nonno by his brother, Antimo. Of the siblings who had immigrated to the USA, Antimo was the only one that returned, subsequently purchasing land on the outskirts of *Orsara* in *Panolino* and *Torre*. The ensemble of their land was exceptionally fertile, always yielding a bountiful harvest. Some villagers even bought seeds from them with the hope of getting the same result. For our area, wheat, grapes and olives were essential. My paternal nonni were very fortunate to produce all three.

My maternal nonni, Paolo and Michelina, lived a few minutes' walk up the street on *Via Dante*. Both were kindhearted, hardworking and generous. They had six children: Franco, Felice, Filomena, Antonetta (Mom), Michele and Maria. Three other children died in their infancy.

Nonna was thin, tall, beautiful and very sociable. Customary to the women of her generation, she wore her long grey hair rolled into a bun on the lower back of her head. She was seldom seen without her long apron with two oversized pockets where she kept her knife ready to pick dandelions or other necessities in her path. She divided her time between the fields, the farm and home. She cured meats, made cheese and canned almost everything the family harvested. Undeniably, her house was one of the most decorated throughout the winter with apple stalks all strung together along the wall, keeping them fresh for a few more months. In her spare time, Nonna Michelina spun yarn on her wheel. The harmony of threads created beautiful hues in socks, scarves and sweaters. Always efficient and fast, she was the queen of winnowing[5] during harvest. She was also known for her remarkably clean laundry. On occasion, some of the wealthier elderly in the village hired her to do their wash.

Nonno Paolo, was tall, thin and held a serious look about him. He was never idle and there was nothing that he could not do, or at least be willing to try. A quiet Renaissance man with many talents. He had worked hard throughout his entire life. Despite a kick by a mule in his young years that had left him limping, he still served in the military. In his post, he transported mules and horses to other soldiers.

My maternal nonno had four siblings: Isabella, Leonardo, Alexandro and Carmino. The three eldest immigrated together to the United States in their teens while Nonno Paolo and Carmino stayed behind to work alongside their parents. His siblings never returned to Italy but for many years, in honor of the *Saint Michele* celebration in September, they sent gift packages with the most beautiful American dresses for Nonno Paolo's girls. One of my mother's

---

[5] Winnowing: Process of separating grain from the shaft during wheat harvest.

favorite was a dark grey silk dress with light grey piping that she had worn when she and Pop eloped. Mom's sister, Felice, had embroidered elegant pink flowers with green leaves on the bodice and along the hemline.

My maternal nonni worked in various fields scattered outside of the village. Additionally, during harvest, Nonno Paolo worked in the fields of others in exchange for crops that they did not grow themselves like the potatoes that filled several wooden crates to the brim. Those precious commodities were tucked under their matrimonial bed.

In *Rapalonge,* the land allocated to Nonno Paolo for his military service, they grew wheat. In their closest field, *Frecchiune*, which was leased from Mrs. Maffei, they repatriated the animals inside the mill during the winter months to afford them some extra warmth. As milk production was also severely reduced during the cold period, Nonna Michelina and the neighboring farmer, who raised cows, agreed to share the milk produced by the cows and goats. They combined all the milk and alternated making cheese during the winter.

During the warmer months, the pigs, sheep and goats grazed the *Dumania* field, the property that my Nonno Paolo had inherited. Most of that land had needed to be cleared before it became useful to them. Although it was a difficult terrain to cultivate, it had a well that kept the animals amply hydrated. Additionally, half of the property had a surplus of fruit trees that allowed Nonna Michelina to routinely fill baskets that the children delivered to neighbors or elderly who were no longer able to work. The rest was all on an incline and unusable for crops. There, Nonno Paolo kept bees which, in the absence of a vineyard, permitted him to trade honey for wine.

On one of Elisa's visits to that orchard, Nonno Paolo had sent her home with a huge basket of big beautiful figs. She insisted that it be carried on her head. Since she was still five years old, he walked her to the edge of the village where they recapped her directions home. He adjusted the twisted rag on her head so she balanced the basket perfectly, just like the grownups. Villagers passing by curiously questioned what she proudly carried on her head. Not knowing how to respond, she offered them the figs. By the time she arrived home, only a handful of figs rolled around the bottom of her basket.

Our family life had changed dramatically after Pop returned from the military. He still helped during the harvest seasons while Mom rarely went. That change was brought forth primarily because of Pop's exposure to the lifestyle in Northern Italy while he served. There, he saw that families did not work all together in the fields from dawn until dusk. Many worked in factories or other businesses that paid steady wages. They were able to buy the things that they needed and their children went to school. That was the life that he had set in his heart for his little family.

In that vein, Pop was fortunate to quickly find a job with *ditta Magiurla,* a contracting company involved with building roads and railways. He mostly dug trenches on the outskirts of the village. Pop's job guaranteed a steady pay that contributed to the prosperity of our growing family as my brother, Alfredo, was born in the spring of 1953. With the nearest hospital being in *Foggia*, mid-wives in the village assisted with child-birth.

Our life on *Via Tasso* felt very comfortable and we always had plenty to eat. Pop rode his bicycle to the job site on the outskirts of the village. My parents also cultivated a small but well-established olive orchard that Pop had inherited from his uncle. Once the trees were pruned, it required very little upkeep. After picking the olives, most of the harvest was taken to a store that had an olive press. We kept some of the olive oil for our everyday necessities and sold or traded the rest for other things. We also reserved some of the olives for our own consumption. To preserve them, we washed, sorted and placed the good ones in a large terracotta or aluminum container. A week later, after the olives started to soften a bit, we seasoned them with salt, garlic and basil. Those delicious olives that macerated slowly in the freshness of our dark and cool cave were available for us to eat year-round.

With Pop's stable income, we had enough money to splurge on a record player that brought so much joy, our home was characterized as the "happy house" by our neighbors. Our door stayed open. On nice Sunday afternoons, the music became an open invitation for them to join us. The furniture was pushed to the side of the room and the ball began.

Our closest friends were recent newcomers to our village, the Simonelli family. Pop and Mr. Simonelli met while they were both in the nearby village of *Troia* for a religious celebration. There, the Bishop had planned to perform the Sacrament of Confirmation for a large group of children from neighboring villages. On a whim, Pop, as an adult, decided to join that group of children who were to receive the sacrament. Mr. Simonelli, one of the volunteers for that event, agreed to sponsor Pop and prepared him in just a few hours.

Upon returning to our village that same day, Pop broke the news to Mom, who had stayed home with the children, that he had been confirmed and had a new godfather. Together, with a pot of coffee in hand and cookies that they bought at the café along the way, my parents walked to their home and celebrated with their new lifelong friends.

Pop and Mr. Simonelli became inseparable. The night of their "godfathers' walk" was one of the most hilarious stories ever told of the two together. On one of their many deep and long conversations over a few glasses of wine, they decided to call it a night. The entire world had already gone to sleep. Their homes were separated by a ten minute walk. Nevertheless, Leonardo Simonelli escorted Pop home. When they reached our home, Pop returned the favor because what kind of person would let the other walk home alone? With more laughter and deep conversation, the men walked one another home for several more hours going well into the night. Fatigued, they agreed to be fair. At mid-distance, they bid their farewell and proceeded to their respective homes. This strange and amusing anecdote was also a testament to how respectfully they treated their friendship throughout their lives. Related by heart and with implicit trust for one another through the best and the worst of times.

We stayed equally close to Pop's sister, Zia[6] Concetta, and her husband, Zio[7] Pellegrino. Our families ate countless meals together. The menu was typically pasta with whatever vegetable had been harvested that day. We shared everything with a genuine sense of conviviality.

One day, Zia had made polenta. Knowing Pop loved it, she brought him some. Elisa, barely six, was cheered on to try it but only grimaced at the sight of it. She didn't trust their taste since they had tricked her before to bite into a raw onion. As always, they eventually swayed her. Elisa found the flavor so repulsive that she instantly grabbed the first thing she saw on the table to drink and remove the dreadful taste from her mouth. Unfortunately, it was an unlabeled glass bottle containing bleach which had been refilled at the store earlier in the day. She instantly began to gag and vomit profusely. Pop tossed her over his shoulder, holding on to her legs tightly as he raced up the hill. Elisa stayed drooped over his back leaving a trail of black vomit all along the road to the clinic situated near the *Saint Angelo* fountain. That upside-down position of her voyage ultimately saved her life.

Not long after, Pop, made the sprint uphill to the clinic again with Elisa in his arms. She was always eager to assist with everything and anything. That day, she intently watched my parents as they made pasta. A sudden cry from the cradle was her calling to rock her baby brother back to sleep. She hastily jumped from the hearth. One foot landed directly into the large pot of scalding pasta water that my parents had placed, out of the way, on the floor next to the fireplace. In shock, instead of withdrawing her foot out of the pot, she planted her other foot inside. Her blisters were so large and deep, the clinician was forced to cut them despite others instantly swelling in their place. Her feet required painful weekly redressing that only Nonna Leonarda was strong enough to tolerate.

Thankfully, after that episode, she stayed far away from the clinic. It took several months of recovery before Elisa walked again and family life resumed

---

[6] Zia: Italian word for Aunt. Zii is plural.
[7] Zio: Italian word for Uncle. Zii is plural.

more normally. We were living in the "happy house" after all. In the rhythm of life, other events, some pleasant while others not so much, followed.

The next generation of our extended family had begun to disperse. On Mom's side, her brother Franco left for Switzerland while her older sisters joined their husbands in Turin where they had found work. On Pop's side, his baby brother, Antimo, barely seventeen years old, immigrated to Venezuela where he had found a job as a mechanic. The husbands of both of his sisters found work in the factories of Turin. They had left alone to work, returning to the village to visit their families from time to time.

The succession of departures was endless. My paternal nonno was next in line to leave us for the United States of America in 1956 under the Refugee Relief Program. His brother, Anzelmo, had secured work for him in the *Luria* steel mill in Bethlehem, a city in the state of Pennsylvania. Nonno's eminent departure was deeply felt by everyone. It was particularly sad for all of his grandchildren who adored him. Their daily ritual to greet him at the *Saint Angelo* fountain upon his return from the fields would be no more. Every day, Nonno Alfredo stopped at the trough by the fountain to let Mr. Baron quench his thirst after a long hard day of toil. The grandchildren were already all assembled there waiting for him. From the fountain, they walked him home together while each grandchild was entitled to their turn to ride Mr. Baron. Elisa was afraid of the mule, so she walked alongside Nonno, her protector. Naturally, when Nonno Alfredo left, he was surrounded by all of his grandchildren on the docks of Naples to bid him farewell and wish him a beautiful adventure to America.

His departure had not only left a huge void in the equilibrium of our family life but also in the fields where work was necessary year round. The trees needed to be pruned after each harvest: the walnut trees at the end of summer and the olive trees in winter. The twigs needed to be collected to make charcoal for cooking and heating our homes. In late winter, the fruit trees were sprayed to avoid diseases that infected the plants and their fruit. Fields were typically plowed by mules, but where the plow could not pass around the trees, it was tilled by hand. At times, when two animals were necessary to pull the plow, it was done in collaboration with others who had similar needs. Spring meant seeding. The men guided the mule and the plow as the women and children followed wearing their aprons with oversized pockets jam-packed with seeds that they threw by the handful between them and the plow. They sowed wheat, beans and chickpeas for the family. For the animals, they planted oats and corn, as corn was not consumed by humans in our area.

There was no shortage of work. Nonna Leonarda was deeply anxious about her field situation. She did not do field work herself so she lacked the skill as well as the desire. To her chagrin, she hired workers by-the-day, but a substantive wheat harvest the following fall was essential so she preferred assistance from someone she trusted. Pop helped whenever he was able, after his regular job, but his mother wished for him to devote himself exclusively to the agricultural work in her wheat field. She asked Pop on several occasions to leave his job and take on the field work. He preferred his formula so he continued to assist while encouraging her to hire daily labor.

As the days became colder, our indispensable portable heater took its place in the center of the room. Mom, aunts and friends always chose chores that gathered them around the source of the warmth. Together, they mended clothes, knit or darned old socks. The men gathered around the table playing card games. The children huddled beside the fireplace together like little chicks in a cozy nest. My brother's favorite spot was almost inside the fireplace. When he did not take refuge in the warmest spot, he mingled with the grown-ups in serious chats about everything and nothing. Irrespective of the season, he was always cold and fatigued. My parents had taken him to the doctor, but his only diagnosis was that he was a little fragile. The doctor recommended the pure mountain air so Elisa or Mom took him to the Pine Forest on nice days.

The arrival of the coldest days heralded the Christmas festivities that were accompanied by the anticipation of preparing the most delicious dishes. Our celebration began on Christmas Eve with linguini prepared with garlic, olive oil, parsley and a dash of salt and pepper. The pièce de résistance for this day was baccala, a Scandinavian dry salt cod. To prepare it, we soaked the filets for nearly two days to remove the excess salt, it was lightly coated with flour, then fried.

The Christmas meal traditionally started with fried dough that we dipped in honey or cooked wine. The other gastronomic specialties were prepared for a dinner that lasted almost an entire day so lunch was not necessary. The dough for the pasta was prepared early, then we collected the other savory foods for our feast. A few dried sausages from the hooks on the ceiling, olives that had been marinating in the cave and fresh mozzarella made up the antipasti. For our favorite winter salad, when we could buy oranges, they were thinly sliced crosswise and seasoned with a touch of garlic, parsley, salt and a drizzle of olive oil.

Our pasta for Christmas day was served with a red meat sauce. It was made with our own preserved tomatoes seasoned with salt, black pepper and parsley, then it simmered for a few hours. We ate meat on special holidays so this sauce was loaded with meatballs and *brasciole*, thinly sliced beef that was seasoned with salt, pepper, parsley, garlic and Romano cheese. They were rolled and tied with some thread to keep from falling apart, fried and added to the sauce to absorb those savors. The dinner would not have been complete without the rabbit and potato roast seasoned with practically all the same wonderful herbs and spices that was taken to the village oven to bake.

We enjoyed course after course and sealed the feast with an assortment of desserts: hard pretzels with anise called *taralli* and my all-time favorite *cauzuncil,*[8] triangular shaped turnovers that were packed with mashed chick peas, cooked wine, lemon zest, grated chocolate and sugar. They were fried with love and served with none other than a drizzle of our cooked wine syrup. The Epiphany[9] on January 6th marked the end of the holidays. To honor that day, little children hung a stocking for the *Befana*. The *Befana,* according to the tale, was an old lady dressed in rags and worn shoes, carrying a sack on her back with toys for good children and coal for those not so good. Although all the children in our family sought the biggest stocking to hang, the *Befana* typically filled them all exactly the same, with an orange and a piece of candy.

In the spring of 1957, my eyes opened to the world. Mr. and Mrs. Simonelli were chosen to be my godparents. They had proposed a name that was not typical for our area, hence the name Olga. Decked out in my white lace christening gown, I was baptized at the church of *San Nicole Di Bari* surrounded by family and friends. It was, once again, a wonderful opportunity to feast and relish in all of the savory aromas of fresh basil, rosemary, parsley and Pecorino Romano cheese. Everyone exuded happiness, meanwhile, my cousin Antonio had a dilemma… He loved pasta, but there were way too many dishes to eat, he could not make any more room in his little belly.

The arrival of springtime heightened Nonna's preoccupation with the work in her wheat field. In order to join Nonno in America, she needed a substantive harvest to finance her trip. In desperation, she offered Pop a very persuasive proposition. If he agreed to leave his construction job and worked exclusively in her wheat field, she would split the profit from the harvest and give him that land before she left the country.

Pop seriously contemplated the proposal for work that he knew well. He reminisced about working with his sister since the age of twelve, alongside Nonno Alfredo. The trio had prepared the soil, plowed, seeded and harvested. Nonno guided the mules to plow, Pop and Zia Concetta trailed behind to seed. By the following season, Pop had already been strong enough to take over the plow. Undeniably, even with Pop secretly stealing a few puffs of cigarette

---

[8] Cauzuncill: Made up *Orsaresi* word for piccolo calzone (small pants).
[9] Epiphany: Christian holiday that commemorates the arrival of the three kings in Bethlehem with gifts for baby Jesus.

behind the straw hut, both he and his sister had not only learned the agricultural work, they had inherited their father's work ethic.

Pop thought long and hard to make the decision responsibly. The wheat field work and its harvest was, by far, the most laborious. It was also the most profitable. Pop also considered the changes in our village. The progress was significant. The roads that were being built around *Orsara* already provided easier access to many of our scattered parcels of land. Fortunately for us, the wheat field was on such a route.

Automation and agricultural services were emerging in our village with machines to thresh and winnow. The silos on the outskirts of town were able to store our wheat so the oversized grain bin in our home was no longer needed. Harvesting had become faster, easier and more lucrative. Even the mules did not need to work quite as hard to thresh, winnow or haul wheat to the village. Rental trucks were available to transport the grain to the silos.

Nevertheless, giving up his job at *ditta Magiurla* after eight years was not a decision that Pop took lightly. He was an excellent employee, accordingly, they encouraged him not to leave. They stated the obvious. The value of jobs with steady pay were few and the lines to get these types of jobs were long. If he quit, it would be near impossible to rehire him. Alone, he carefully weighed his options. Ignoring all of the advice against it by most around him, he accepted his mother's proposition. From his point of view, his decision to work the land was reasonable, prudent and viable. Most importantly, he saw it as a good opportunity for the future of his family.

Pop and Mr. Baron journeyed the five miles to the wheat field every day. The reaping was still done manually using a sickle in one hand and pieces of wild cane inserted on each fingertip of the other hand to lengthen the grip. The pieces were cut to roughly four to six inches in length and set just above the knuckle, so as not to impede hand and finger movement. The elongated hand allowed for better manipulation of larger quantities of wheat at a faster rate.

With the help of Mr. Baron, Pop plowed, seeded, reaped and finally stacked all of the wheat in large piles. He loaded the grain in a rental truck for transport to the village where it would be threshed and winnowed. Arriving at the silo after closing, he unloaded the truck and slept near the grain. Pop's work was done, the day of promise had arrived.

His mother met him at the shop as soon as it opened to handle the sale. The grain was weighed and she was paid. She pocketed the money, all of the profit, then she left him planted in the street like a stranger without saying a single word. The message was clear. He had worked an entire year but there would be no money, no harvest, and no land for our future.

Pop, who had always strived to stay ahead of improving our tomorrows, was shattered beyond belief by that unexpected posturing. Without the revenue from wheat harvest, we were ruined. Nevertheless, he did not have the time to dwell on an un-kept promise. Instead, he focused on the things that were essential. Our money had run out. He was concerned that my brother continued to feel under the weather. There were five of us, plus a mule, who would need to eat over the course of the following year. Those resolutions were his priority.

As for his options, he was painfully aware that he had zero chance of returning to *ditta Magiurla*. That ship had not only sailed, it had sunk and the oars had floated away. Other than the small olive orchard, we had no productive land of our own. But even with land, harvest was over. Working for others by-the-day was a way of the past. The newly built roads, along with the arrival of machinery in our village, significantly reduced the need for daily labor. Even if manual labor was available, it would not happen before spring. Over the years, some of my uncles had tried to persuade Pop to go to the factories in Northern Italy alone, but he always declined in favor of living in the village as a family. Those jobs had become hard to get as well. Given our situation, there was no hope, our fate in the village was sealed. The prospects for finding a positive outcome to this situation were less than meek with time quickly running out.

Regardless of the circumstance, even making the wrong choice was better than doing nothing. Several weeks later, Pop visited a friend, Giuseppe, who worked in France. He was in town for a few weeks on a family visit. Over a cup of espresso, he asked the million dollar question, "Tell me, Giuseppe. Can I go to France?" The reply was instantaneous, "Yes. Of course." Giuseppe Cericola was a recruiter for the *Office of National Immigration (ONI).*[10] Pop was strong and unafraid of hard work. He was an excellent candidate that Mr. Cericola could easily guarantee. He helped Pop with the employment contract as well as all of the associated logistics to work in a coal mine with the *Anzin Company*[11] in Northern France. His start date was set for November 18, 1958.

With that, he broke the news to Mom. He vowed that the arrangement would be temporary. We needed to eat, this plan allowed him to send us money. When life became more comfortable for our family, he would return to *Orsara* with enough money to buy land of our own. It was a chance for a fresh start. He stressed that our life would be better but better would not be easy.

---

[10] *Office of National Immigration (ONI):* In existence since 1945 servicing labor in France after WWII. The organization selected the best candidates that best fit their demands principally in the demand for labor in the coal mines in the Nord of France.

[11] *Anzin* Company: Founded in 1757. One of the oldest mines established in France. The mine, working condition and lives of the families are portrayed in Emile Zola's Germinal of 1885.

Mom was entirely dissatisfied, but he only had days before his departure and there was much to do. What they did agree on was that neither of my parents had ever borrowed money and all options involved going into debt. Without a miracle, it would take forever to get out of debt if we did borrow money. Already, we were unable to pay a small tab with our name at the local grocer. Given no other choice, they borrowed just enough to cover the cost for food and other incidentals for our family until he was able to send money.

On November 15, we were all at the *Orsara* train station to bid a sad farewell to Pop. He did not know what to expect in the coal mine of Northern France, the place where he saw hope. We knew it would be another year before we saw one another again. Over his twenty hour journey over the course of two days to the Nord[12] he unceasingly reminded himself of his words to Mom, "It is an opportunity and it is temporary. We will be together again."

In the Nord, he was welcomed into one of the many barracks for men who were single or separated from their families. Some of the buildings had served as prisons during the war. Pop was assigned to a unit in one of several long rows of barracks in a secluded area that sat on dirt roads. Everything was completely covered with black dust, the signature of the mining cities of the Nord.

Each dwelling was shared by four men. It included a common room with a sink and tap for cold water, a coal stove for heating and cooking, and a table with four chairs. The bedroom had four cots and a small coal stove for added heat during cold nights. All of the men shared a bathroom outside.

Day after day, he boarded the bus alongside his comrades at the end of the road. They shuttled together to and from the mine of *Agache* in *Fenain*. At the mine, Pop followed the queue to pick up his lamp and protective hat which some years later was modified to include a headlamp. It avoided having to carry the extra weight of the lamp and their batteries to keep them lit throughout the day. Then he climbed into the cage. Arms tucked in, he descended approximately two thousand feet underground. Down in the pit of the earth with a pic and a sledge hammer, he crawled into places so tight that a human being could barely hold himself even in a tightly curled up position. By the end of the day, they had all camouflaged to the black dust surrounding them, only their eyes were identifiable with their voices as signature. The cage returned them to the earth only once per day, at the end of their shift.

---

[12] Nord: France is divided into 101 department and 18 regions. The Nord is a department in the Hauts-de-France region in France. It is surrounded by French departments Pas-de-Calais and Aisne, Belgium and the North Sea.

Pop showered daily at the mine then shuttled back to the barracks. Along with his companions, they sat under the blue sky for as long as they could to breathe fresh air. Every two weeks, Pop bought food from a grocer in a truck, *Piccolo*, another Italian immigrant. Pop shared the cost of groceries along with meals with his barrack mates.

The language barrier was oftentimes challenging for immigrants but not for Pop. He was very sociable. If there was a fellow Italian *paisano* to help translate, great, otherwise he was not bashful to make himself understood, undoubtedly using gestures or words that didn't exist in any language. He cared more about being understood than being correct.

Except for money essential for food and some incidentals, Pop sent the bulk of his earnings to his family in *Orsara*. Money arrived from France within a month. As a priority, Mom repaid our debts. His countless letters that arrived every few days had every bit of space blackened with a collection of beautiful stories. He never complained. According to Pop, he was always fine. He wrote about the abundance of work and the friends that he had made so we also came to know whom he shared his stories with.

That year was the first time that the holidays came and went unnoticed. In early December 1958, Nonna joined Nonno Alfredo in America. Pop had left for France a few weeks earlier. We did not accompany the rest of the family to the docks of Naples to say goodbye to Nonna Leonarda.

In January, the village doctor was still unable to determine the cause of my brother's persistent weakness. After much ado from Mom, along with the help of my godfather, Mr. Simonelli, medical care was arranged. My brother was admitted at the *Reuniti Hospital* in *Foggia*. Over the winter, Mom and my brother had short stays at the hospital which required long trips. There was a daily taxi that travelled the twenty-five miles from *Orsara* to *Foggia*. For us, it was unaffordable so Mom spent her nights at the hospital in *Foggia*.

By many turns of unfortunate events, life forced Elisa into becoming a little mommy long before her time. She was almost nine years old and although no one had charged her with this job, she stopped going to school and took care of me. I was seven months old. Our neighbor, Mr. Biondo, checked in on us from time to time. He took Elisa to the fountain and taught her to wash our clothes. During bad storms, he slept on the floor in our house so we would not be afraid.

Our mornings knew the same ritual. Having refused all offers for milk from other mothers who were nursing their babies, Elisa beat an egg and sugar mixture that we dunked bread into for breakfast. We began our tour with a walk to the Pine Forest. Elisa carried me on her back which forced her to make frequent stops because of my heftiness. Then, we met our cousins at Zia Concetta's house. She was almost always out working in the fields. To pass the time, we all paraded to *Cibella*, the blacksmith. They cleaned up his rusty nails while I mostly watched or napped. We pooled our collection of the better quality nails and sold it to vendors who came regularly from other villages to buy metal as well as other recyclable items. We often played ball that we had made ourselves with old rags that were tightly wrapped since we didn't have a real one.

Oftentimes in the evening, dinner was with Zia Concetta, otherwise Elisa prepared *pastina* for us at home. It was the tiniest of pasta that took a minute to cook in boiling water. As soon as it came off the stove, she added a dash of salt, then dropped an egg in it. Whatever we did, we were joined at the hip or I was on her back. Every now and then, some of our aunts tried to separate us so she could play outside alone to regain some freedom. But, between my screaming on one side of the door and her crying on the other side, it did not take long before they unlocked the door as we immediately fell into each other's arms.

In between visits home from the hospital, my brother continuously talked about his fantasy for when he would be old enough to partake in Holy Communion. Fascinated with every aspect of the celebration for this Sacrament, he imagined himself wearing a white suit and having a plethora of white confetti candy wrapped in vibrant tissue paper for all of his guests. He loved the sugar coated almond shaped candy that was often offered as a wedding party favor.

Unfortunately, in March his health significantly deteriorated. That time, my brother remained in the *Reuniti* hospital for an exceptionally long time. Our only communication with Mom over those forty days was through a taxi driver who made daily rounds at the entrance of the hospital and *Foggia's* main square, *Piazza Lanza*. The driver was a trusted friend of our family. When Mom had messages for Elisa, she waited for the taxi driver at his designated arrival time at the hospital. When Mom needed money for various expenses or food, Elisa gave it to the driver who brought it to Mom in *Foggia* the next day. Elisa also passed on the letters that arrived from Pop. As Mom remained in *Foggia* for so long, she sometimes spent nights at the home of a friend who lived near the hospital. For her hospitality, Mom paid her host with olive oil, wheat and beans. The things that everyone needed.

Immediately after Pop had left, Elisa had begun to manage the money that he wired from France to the Post Office in *Orsara*. She knew to hide the money in the clock's secret compartment on top of the buffet. Barely able to reach the top of the cabinet, she climbed a stool mounted on top of a wooden crate. She diligently kept records for all of her purchases: milk, eggs or *pastina*.

Occasionally, she bought bananas because I loved them, a piece of candy or an ice cream cone for us to share. Elisa was very well known by the shop owners where we were always met with the greatest kindness. Time and again, they offered us food or candy but she only accepted what she could pay for.

After six weeks, my brother began to feel stronger. He was eager to return home in time to participate in the procession for *Saint Michele* on May 8. He said it was his duty to participate because *Saint Michele* and Pop carried the same first name. Pop's name was *Michelino*. It was not exactly the same but close enough for him to call it "Pop's day." A few days later, when the procession passed our house, he proudly took his place among the children.

Unfortunately, in the ensuing days he weakened more and more. He and Mom made their last trip to *Reuniti Hospital*. By early morning, my brother had joined the other angels in paradise. That day, a nurse, a friend and a taxi driver had all taken great risks to help Mom honor my brother's last wish to return home. Because he had died in the hospital, he would not be released. Instead, his death was never recorded and Mom managed to get falsified discharge papers.

A woman Mom had befriended at the hospital was almost always there with her ill sister. She kept guard on my brother while Mom quickly sent a telegram to notify Pop in France knowing that it would cause her to miss the taxi departure time to return to *Orsara*. Her friend offered to negotiate Mom's return trip with another driver. Since her shoes hurt her feet, Mom took hers off and gave them to her friend to walk faster. Once everything was organized, Mom quickly wrapped my brother in a blanket. As calmly as possible, she passed the security post at the exit of the hospital to join her taxi at the designated location. She stood, waiting for a long time, still not noticing that she was no longer wearing shoes. The planned taxi never arrived while another driver instantly declined her request once he took a quick glance under the blanket.

Hopeless, with heaviness in her heart, she noticed an empty carriage parked nearby. Completely drained, she climbed in and simply sat to ponder over what to do next. The driver of the carriage eventually spotted her but was also alarmed as he quickly assessed the state of affairs. Sensing her deep grief, he wanted to offer assistance but it was impossible for him to make the long trip by horse and carriage. Instead, he drove Mom to *Piazza Lanza* where he negotiated a ride for her. Similar to the other drivers, he was worried about losing his license if what she had done was discovered. Mom was desperate so she promised the driver that she would be strong and would not cry for the entire trip to *Orsara*. In profound silence, holding her heart tightly in her arms, they traveled the twenty-five miles. When Mom arrived home, still barefoot, she carried my brother up the steep incline to our street, laid him on the bed, and then evenly asked Elisa to pay the driver. Finally, the agony in her broken heart could no longer be contained. Elisa too was struck by shock and immense grief as she realized the enormity of the situation. That day, the small bell tolled for my brother.

According to the traditions of that time, last respects were at home. A headboard, created by a white sheet covered in ivy was placed at the head of our table. For my brother, we added strings of white confetti candy. Mom's rose satin bedspread was draped over our kitchen table in the center of the room where the small casket was resting. The little man rested in a pure white silk suit that a family friend had sewn for him and he was wholly surrounded by white confetti candy.

The funeral was delayed until Pop arrived from France. From the train station on the outskirts of the village, Pop ran the distance directly to the cemetery where the family was already waiting for him. In the deepest raw pain, Pop embraced his little boy one last time.

The tragedy had been completely unforeseen by anyone. It seemed impossible to survive as a family. Pop desperately sought for any path forward from this inextricably difficult situation. During his week in *Orsara*, he pleaded with Mom to go to France with him but she refused to leave my brother behind. Any courage or strength that she had found to return my brother home from the hospital had died and was buried with him. She was completely lost and very fragile. A shattered Pop returned to France alone to salvage his job. He was only six months into a one-year contract without leave.

The *Anzin Company* allowed Pop to establish another contract for a year. He hoped that it would also provide time to allow his family to come to France. In the meantime, he worried about us being alone in *Orsara* for yet another year. Pop immersed himself in his job. His life had become very dark both underground and above ground. For as much as he detested being alone, he spent the most difficult days of his life in the barracks of the Nord grieving and suffering in solitude. We, in *Orsara,* had the comfort of the Simonelli family who never left our side. They had also become part of Pop's voice echoing his countless letters that pleaded with Mom to give the Nord a chance. They said, "We needed to be whole with Pop…Perhaps an opportunity to start healing existed in the Nord." Time after time, she refused.

The following months remained infinitely dark and painful. Our family was not only apart, we were very broken. The pink satin bedspread was carefully folded and put away, never to be used again. Mom spent almost all of her time in the cemetery near her lost heart, attempting to collect herself. Elisa and I were alone again. More than ever, she remained my attentive little mommy.

31

Pop's determination never wavered. After countless letters exchanged, Mom finally agreed to join Pop in France after All Saints Day.

The grief and despair was intense as Mom tried to think about other matters related to our imminent departure. Between her daily visits to the cemetery and the help of a friend, Mom sewed two dresses as well as two pairs of pants for me and Elisa who were both in growth spurts. She also knitted wool sweaters for the cold winter ahead. We even took a bus to the big city of *Troia* where we bought new shoes for all of us.

When November 17, 1959 arrived, Elisa was relieved to leave the place that had filled with sadness and painful memories. She also missed Pop. Still too young to have an opinion, I was perfectly happy to go wherever my little mommy decided to go.

Our suitcases were packed with our necessities: a few clothes, some pictures, our linens, Mom's American dress and what had become the sacred rose satin bedspread. Our house was left intact as if we were simply going on a vacation.

We boarded the train in *Orsara* with my godfather, Leonardo Simonelli, who accompanied us all the way to Milan to ensure our transfer went well. At two years old, my world view made the train station in Milan an amusement park, although we had never seen one of those either. All around us, we discovered charming shops full of so many toys that we didn't know existed. Most impressive of all were the escalators that were so long they seemed to touch the sky. Poor Elisa! Hand in hand, we spent hours riding up and down those modern machines.

In the evening, my godfather helped us to board a train that, in the following ten hours, would be taking us to a new horizon in France.

3

The Nord: Hornaing – City Heurteau (Part 1)

Screeching brakes awakened us in the wee hours of the morning. My sister and I excitedly looked forward to our new life in the new world that Pop had written to us about. A few minutes sufficed to organize our belongings so we were ready to quickly exit the train at the next stop. We ate the last of our snacks that we had packed in a little satchel for this trip. Mom, deep in thought, was seated in the same spot on the cot as the night before, gazing at the same photo of my brother that rested in her lap. At some point during the night, she had inserted it into a pretty wooden frame that my godfather had helped her to choose while we waited for our transfer in Milan. The brakes shrieked one last time as the knock on our compartment door announced our stop in *Valenciennes*.

Our excitement swiftly moved us off the train where we found Pop's warm arms. No doubt he had rushed the large crowd to find us. He held us so tight as if for almost an eternity then glanced toward the photo in Mom's hand. There was no need for words, the collective faces flooded with tears.

Pop had picked us up with his friend Tomas who owned a car. Tomas and his family, who had left *Orsara* some years earlier, now lived in the *Camu*, a mine community in *Douai*.

That day marked another sequence of firsts. My first car ride! Curious and a little scared, my face stayed glued to the car window mesmerized by everything along the road. We were on our way to our new home in a small community called *City Heurteau*[13] situated just across the railroad tracks in the

---

[13] *City Heurteau*: Mine housing established in 1927 at the same time as the mine of Heurteau..

north of *Hornaing*[14] that Pop's letters had already told us consisted of four rooms!

Since our home would not be ready for another day, we arrived at the home of Pop's friends, Guillermo and Zurla. The couple had emigrated from Sicily several years prior. Upon entering their home, Pop's eyes welled again as he inhaled the aroma that wafted in the air. It was apparent that Zurla had prepared an Italian feast for our arrival!

Tightening my grip on Elisa's hand, my eyes followed Pop, whom I found had all the appearance of warmth. He was a stranger to my eyes but not my heart. Shortly after our arrival, he disappeared momentarily, then he reemerged with a doll that stood taller than me. Her chestnut hair was separated into braids that were decorated with a pink bow on each side of her warm smile and sparkling eyes. She wore a lovely white lace dress with light pink piping around the collar, hem and cuffs. One of Pop's companions who had won the doll at the *ducasse*[15] a few months earlier, had given it to him in anticipation of his little girl coming to France. Although Pop had already conquered my heart at the train station, he completely won me over when he placed that gigantic doll in my arms. Incapable of containing himself, he revealed his real surprise. A tricycle for me and a bicycle for Elisa which were to arrive in the ensuing days.

After dinner, we strolled on the pavers[16] of our new neighborhood. We stopped as we neared the end of *Rue de Donzere* to admire the end unit of a row of six homes. Our new home! The red brick houses all resembled one another. A slight variation between red and white bricks framed the front doors and windows. It was obvious to me that this distinction was intentional to allow small children like me to find their home. The windows were all protected by wooden shutters that were closed at dusk to keep the houses warmer and reopened to the sunshine early in the morning.

Similar to the cluster of homes that made up *City Heurteau*, a short wooden gate provided access into our small courtyard. Remnants of the fall hues and foliage were still popping all around our house. On the left of the six cement steps leading to our front door, a tiny recess in the wall gave way directly into our basement. Pop had already told us that we would have enough coal to cook and to keep our house well-heated. The mine regularly delivered a mound of

---

[14] *Hornaing*: Town situated in the Nord (Pas-de-Calais Region), department of *Hauts de France*, approximately 36 Km northeast of Lille (capital) and 182 Km from Paris. Before the mines opened, *Hornaing* was predominantly an agricultural area specializing in grain and sweet beets.
[15] Ducasse: Carnival.
[16] Pavers: The "pavers" of the Nord, were characteristic of the roads of that region, a covering of sandstone cubes (sandstone-flint) manually assembled on a bed of sand.

pellets, as well as a mound of coal dust to all their workers. All free! The tiny pellets of coal were all hard-pressed to the size of an egg. The dust was coal residue that had been reduced to powder. Combined, they made an excellent fuel. All we had to do was to shovel this precious fuel into the basement through the hole in the wall.

Pop pointed to an enormous building adjacent to our home that appeared abandoned, stressing we were never to approach it. Two towering headframes intended to descend beneath the earth stood behind it. Although no coal had ever been mined there, it was known as the mine of *Heurteau*. Its function was limited to serve as ventilation for the mine at *Agache* where Pop worked. Much of the mine terrain was occupied by *La Centrale,* a coal-fired power plant that included a huge red and white striped smoke stack along with two giant round refrigerants. Coupled, they cooled the water to be reused for the proper operation of the electric turbines.

Observing us in the street, the Krawczyk family came outside to welcome us to the neighborhood. Mr. Krawczyk was an engineer at *La Centrale.* Accordingly, he was allotted the attractive huge single home situated directly across the street from ours where he lived with his wife and their three children: Nellie, Shantal and Gilles. Pointing to the swing and the wooden seesaw in their charmingly manicured yard, Nellie offered me an open invitation to come and play.

We inspected every part of our new home. Pop, time and again, had told us that it was identical to that of Guillermo and Zurla, but we wanted to see it for ourselves. It was huge and it had windows that actually opened! A coal stove in the corner of the common room and another in the kitchen would surely keep us warm. The doll which accompanied me everywhere, took her seat in the center of the large green sofa bed where she could be admired each and every day. The sofa bed and a sewing machine, a surprise for Mom, were the only items that Pop had purchased as new.

In the kitchen, a buffet rested beside a staircase leading to two bedrooms while a table and six chairs occupied the rest of that space. All of those items, plus our beds and an armoire were purchased second hand from the previous owner. Actually, it was a trade. The gentlemen who vacated the house was paying back on a loan from Pop. The furniture was not made of walnut from Nonno Paolo's trees but it suited our family perfectly. The sink in the kitchen was magical! Pop seized every opportunity to turn the faucet on and off, just to hear me laugh. Mom was thrilled too. No more water chores at the fountain with barrels on her head, or back and forth to do our laundry on cold or rainy days. The happiest of all was Elisa who, after a thorough inspection, was fully satisfied that our house was not equipped with a stall which guaranteed Mr.

Baron would not be joining us. He would live happily ever after exactly where he was!

Our very own toilet was outside on the back porch. The porch descended onto a large garden planted with purple iris and tons of golden hues. Living on the last street of the mine community offered us a picture-perfect view of the huge pasture that was adorned year-round with an array of rich colors for each of their seasons for as far as we could see. Cows and horses grazed throughout. Separating our yard from the pasture was a narrow dirt path that led to a forest on the right.

To lessen Mom's apprehension about getting around town easily and comfortably by bus, Pop took her on a trial trip to the open market in *Somain*. There, they bought groceries plus a few other incidentals for our home. Wandering through the marketplace, a table decked with pretty white lace caught Mom's eye. They bought enough to sew curtains for our entire home with Mom's brand new sewing machine.

While our parents shopped, we pretended to be princesses in our little castle until a sudden knock at the door startled us. Unable to speak a word of French, magnified by not knowing anyone, Elisa guardedly cracked the door open. There, she stood face-to-face with several girls wearing big smiles, unmistakably welcoming her to the neighborhood: Christiane, Chantal, Evelyn, Dolores while Jean Pierre waved from the street on his bicycle. From that day forward, they all remained inseparable. That marked our first two perfect days in *City Heurteau*!

We were told that Pop had rejuvenated the day that he held us in his arms on the train platform in *Valencienne*. His many friends wanted to meet his long anticipated family. One day, a comrade arrived by car to accompany us to the barracks, Pop's previous abode.

In conversation, Elisa revealed her distress over riding a bicycle. Another companion who had overheard instantly resolved her dilemma. His bicycle had a bar that she was not quite tall enough to put her leg over. Determined, she crouched underneath the bar mastering it before we left the barracks that day. The following day, a shiny red tricycle and a yellow bicycle arrived at our front door for me and my sister. Both appeared to have been well cared for by their previous owners.

With all the kindness and generosity, it did not take long to integrate within our new community. Our remarkable neighbors and friends all looked out for one another. Zurla helped Mom to set up daily deliveries for milk and bread. The milk truck that made its rounds early each morning placed ours on the window sill. For our bread, Mom occasionally liked to bake bread in the convenience of her very own oven at home. She was beyond thrilled to have such choices! The bread truck typically arrived in the early afternoon. It did not linger in one place for too long as they had countless stops to make around the neighborhoods. To avoid missing our pickup, especially on cold wintry days when the pavers on the streets were wet and slick, we kept a pair of old socks near the door to quickly pull over our shoes to keep us from slipping.

Likewise, it did not take long to acclimate to the Saturday morning ritual of living in a coal town. Our walkways were scrubbed with soapy water to remove the dark grey film coating it. Even the laundry cords needed to be cleaned before hanging the wash that Mom was elated to do using her own washing machine. The machine did not spin but Mom did not care. Thursdays and Saturdays were the designated laundry days, sometimes more often, depending on when Pop brought his work clothes from the mine. Terrified of ruining the machine with those virtually unrecognizable filthy clothes, Mom hand-washed them first to remove as much of the coal residue as possible, then she rewashed them by machine.

The sewing machine was almost always in use. Mom's work was well advertised by our clothes as well as the lace curtain draped over the front window. In no time at all, she was recognized as an expert seamstress with impeccable perfectionism in our community.

Elisa entered the School for girls on *Rue Paul Lafargue* in *Hornaing*. She cycled to and from school every day with her new friends. Her anxiety about starting a new school had significantly lessened by her new friendships, although she was deeply annoyed to have been placed in the first grade with younger children to learn the language. Nevertheless, between school and her friends, she learned to speak French very quickly. By the following autumn, she advanced to the second grade, then she advanced one grade with each quarter. By the end of that school year, she was delighted to be promoted to her appropriate level in the same fourth grade class with her friends.

Pop always looked for even the smallest ways to make us happy. One day, he brought me two cardboard boxes filled with a miniature wooden house and tiny furniture. All handmade! He said he wanted us to have real toys. At the same time, he and Mom made up for lost time. On weekends, they owned the dance floor at the Dancing Café beside the railroad tracks on *Rue Jean Duez*. Their happiness transformed our home into the "happy house" filled with friends on most Sunday afternoons.

Pop had also recruited enough community interest to merit a stop from the Italian grocery truck, *Piccolo*. Making it my job to enthusiastically announce the truck's arrival, I leaped onto the narrow step behind the truck after *Piccolo* rolled up the aluminum door for a front row view of many Italian foods that were unfamiliar to our neighbors. My favorite part was hearing Pop describe the assortment of cheeses and cured sausages suspended all around the truck. We bought blocks of parmesan and Romano cheese that we grated ourselves to sprinkle on almost everything we ate. In the event we ran out before *Piccolo* returned, the Decommer Farm, which was a short walk past the *Passage a Niveau,* was our standby.

From *Piccolo,* we also bought box pasta and hard candy, mostly for me and Pop. He did not have a sweet tooth like me, he enjoyed a piece of hard candy after work to get that bitter taste of coal out of his mouth. *Piccolo* always ran promotions. One in particular was gigantic silverware. The forks and spoons were so oversized, they could easily have been mistaken for serving utensils. Our parents were quite excited about them and, over time, collected the full matching set. Elisa and I always opted for the old un-matched smaller ones.

Our fresh fruits and vegetables came from the open market in *Hornaing.* In the spring of 1960, Pop transformed our backyard into a gorgeous edible garden that excited our appetite and satisfied any afternoon craving. He planted tomatoes, cucumbers, Swiss chard, green beans, peas and zucchini. Stone pathways had been created throughout the entire garden. A combination of flowers and wild strawberries served as a border. A variety of fruit trees such as peaches, cherries, mulberries and apricots shared their space. Gladiolas and dahlias, planted by a former occupant, appeared as if they had been intentionally woven into the garden.

Everything of necessity was easily accessible by foot, bicycle or bus. Our school, a general store, a café and a church were all within a short walk. Transport to work for Pop at the mine of *Agache* in *Fenain* remained by the company shuttle. His stop was at the bar down the street near the Dancing Café.

As nicer days approached with the onset of our first spring in *City Heurteau,* Pop was eager to teach Mom how to ride a bicycle. He thought she would appreciate getting around town to run her errands more independently. Our practices on the path between the pasture and our house were a true family affair!

As an expert tri-cyclist, I provided moral support. Mom was uncoordinated, terrified of cycling and still unstable on two wheels after several weeks. Although Pop was never one to give up, he eventually accepted her preference to walk or take the bus wherever she needed to go. As an alternative, Pop bought a light blue mobylette[17] that permitted him to travel longer distances with Mom as a passenger. It was another occasion to spend more time in the

---

[17] Mobylette: Moped by Motobecane Company.

pure air under the blue sky. On nice days, he took his moped to work and always took the time to offer me and Elisa rides after work.

Our new life suited me well, although it came with new parental rules and an enormous adjustment with the absence of Elisa by my side all the time. She went to school every day. She was a good student and adored her teachers. Elisa kept the time with her friends sacred without jeopardizing her responsibilities at home after school. She wisely learned that taking me along meant more time with her friends. My place was in the passenger seat behind Elisa.

All together, we rode through the woods breathing in the fragrant pines, honeysuckle and lily of the valley. A satchel underneath my seat with pockets that hung on each side of the back wheel came in handy to store any nuts that we had picked along the way as a surprise for Mom. When the goose berries, blackberries, raspberries, mulberries or whatever was in season ripened, they filled the basket suspended from the handle bar.

The silly new rules imposed were attributed to the fact that my parents were not fully familiar with the area and did not know everyone in town as they had in our little village of *Orsara*. The strict rules imposed were obviously non-negotiable. On the occasion that we found ourselves outside of the permissible boundary, which was not far at all, Elisa always stopped at the candy store to buy me a creamy strawberry coconut *boule* on our way home. Beside chocolate, that soft coconut boule had made my list of favorite sweets so there was no need to question her motives. Still, with or without candy, buying my silence was not necessary. Simply being with my sister was enough.

Our long anticipated *Ducasse* arrived in the summer of 1960. With bated breath, my sister and I walked hand-in-hand to the carnival that covered the entire grounds of the *Heurteau Chapel*. Lucky at the roulette, Elisa won a rooster after a few rounds. Needless to say, our adventure was cut short. The rooster was not particularly pleased about this situation either, but we needed to get him into our chicken coop at home. There, perhaps he would settle down upon meeting a few new friends. It was not the first time Elisa had handled such a feathered friend. One hand held the rooster upside down by its feet, the other hand held on to mine.

Over the next few days, strutting his handsome colors as he saw fit, he assumed the role of guarding a flock of chickens. Except for his cock-a-doodle-doos at the crack of dawn, he was fairly entertaining. Unbeknownst to him, he was joining us for Sunday dinner with our friends in *Douai*.

When Tomas arrived to pick us up, we hurried to his car while Pop took charge of the rooster. As Pop approached the coop, the seriously guarded rooster defiantly flew higher than expected. The open top guaranteed the rooster his freedom toward the pasture. Clearly he had a vision of his destiny later that day in close proximity of roasted potatoes. Elisa and I were doubled over laughing while the grownups all busily chased a rooster who was clearly determined to find a different path for his future. Nearly an hour later, the rooster finally lost some steam which allowed Pop to apprehend it on the path to the forest. Tuckered out, we all rode to the mine community in Douai called the *Camu* from where the rooster did not return.

In autumn, Mom took me with her to *Orsara* over All Saints Day. Pop had unequivocally rejected any notion for himself to ever return to our village and Elisa could not miss school.

We stayed in our home on *Via Tasso*. It was exactly as we had left it the year prior. Each morning we visited my brother's grave. Upon entering the metal gates of the cemetery, Mom guided me down a concrete stairwell that led to a mausoleum. She silently walked away toward my brother's gravesite for her deep painful moments of recollection. In my space, I waited as quiet as a mouse until she returned for our solemn walk home.

Our family had readily voiced their discontent concerning my absent Italian vocabulary. On the flipside, it did not affect my afternoons which were filled with tons of chatter, fun and games with all of my cousins. We spent some time with my godparents who had recently opened a *tabacchi* store in a tiny borough outside of *Orsara* where they also resided. Mr. and Mrs. Simonelli had four children: Enza, Lucia, Carmela and Mario. They all treated me like a princess.

One evening, I was alone with Enza and Lucia while they managed the store. Being a chatterbox, the babbling, of nothing important, in French was nonstop. They tried to understand me, but it was a lost cause. Instead, they offered me chocolate. As a lover of chocolate, it was accepted without question. A lot of it! The nurse that made a house visit that night assessed that my convulsions were related to consuming way too much chocolate! The situation was remedied by a concoction of crushed garlic paste intended to quickly induce vomiting. Needless to say, even the word "chocolate" was forbidden to roll from my lips for the rest of our stay.

Before we knew it, our two weeks had passed. We boarded our train just down the road from the home of my godparents for another adventure back to *City Heurteau*. Our compartment was crowded with several large burlap sacks filled with wool that Mom was transporting to refill our mattresses. She had removed it from the mattresses in our home in *Orsara* and washed it in the canal with the aid of my godmother, Enza and Lucia. It had taken a full week for the wool to dry before they stuffed it into the sacks.

Mom slept well during this train ride but, for me, my curiosity was always stronger than my sleepiness. Tiptoeing as quiet as a mouse out of our compartment into the deserted corridors to follow sounds of faint singing eventually took me to its source. A car crowded with very excited young people rang with patriotic songs. Settled into the lap of one of the protesters, my chants matched theirs: *Kubasi, Khrushchev. Kubasi, Khrushchev.* Barely three, their words were meaningless but my new friends were kind and taught me the jingles. By the wee hours of the morning, Mom appeared in the doorway with one of the conductors. Her gaze alternated between angry and happy. She thanked my new friends for taking care of me, then scooped me away.

In the privacy of our cabin, she forbid me to leave it in her unmistakably clear tone. With nothing else left to do, my attention shifted toward the spectacular soaring mountains completely covered by a pure white blanket of snow from top to bottom. My face was pressed on the window simply awe-struck by the beauty of the Alps that remained permanently engraved in my memories.

For my countless stories told in *Orsara* about France, plenty more were ready to share with our friends in *City Heurteau* about my Italy. Tales about the pigs tied to the front door of some homes and the *fucacoste* that burned in all of the streets, captivated my audience. Hearing about the mules that ate and slept in our house made their eyes grow wider.

Nothing was left out! Not even the animal feces that peppered the streets, some of which had soiled my brand new light blue coat after slipping just outside of our front door. Pop, beyond aghast, made numerous attempts to discreetly redirect the conversation, but I was unstoppable. Luckily for him, my vocabulary lacked the words to adequately describe how we lived. He resolved to assist me with a translation that painted a considerably lovelier picture.

City Heurteu truly had become our land of promise as evidenced by the day following the Epiphany in January 1961. The *Befana* had made a special delivery for us, a baby brother named Alfredo Salvatore. It was a delightful surprise, although, it seemed to me that the *Befana* had been somewhat careless. The package with my baby brother was certainly more fragile than her other gifts. It seemed reasonable to me that she should have delivered him as a priority, before dropping off gifts to all of the other good children, not the day after Epiphany!

A month later, we celebrated the baptism for our little newcomer. Nellie, across the street was his godmother. In keeping with our *Saint Anthony* traditions, when Alfredo Salvatore turned one, he wore the customary habit that Mom had sewn for the benediction. Since it fell on a weekday, she and I accompanied my brother to the *Heurteau Chapel,* then we strolled to the studio in *Hornaing* for his photos.

In autumn 1962, my entrance to kindergarten at *Suzanne Lanoy* was fabulous but short lived. The walk to school was not long, then again, distance was not my problem. The bedroom shared with my sister was the darkest room in the universe. Thankfully, we only went there to sleep. To hide from its chilling blackness, my head stayed under the protection of the sheets and blankets. From time to time, Elisa awakened during the night to pull me out from the foot of the bed deep under the covers. To my dismay, she left for her school prior to my waking. Stealing a quick glimpse over the blanket verified that it was still dark. The light switch was never an option since it compelled me to get out of bed in the dark. Mom, assuming her little girl was too tired, allowed me to sleep. This arrangement suited me just fine!

On those intermittent school days, Mom prepared my favorite breakfast. A mixture of egg and milk slightly sweetened and beaten, a slice of toast coated by a thin layer of orange marmalade, and a cup of warm milk flavored with a spoonful of espresso coffee. My shortcut to *Suzanne Lanoy* was alongside the fence surrounding the immense headframes of the mine. The long flat-roofed building nearby that Pop had forbidden us to approach resembled old attached garages. Although workers had never been seen there, their huge doors were occasionally left open.

Drawn there while trying to be mindful of Pop's warnings, only a guarded sneak peek inside the entrance sufficed. Stairs alongside that structure led to a narrow overpass to someplace not easily seen. The bright red "do not enter" letters on the sign attached to the fence surrounding that area settled any decision on my part. When fear completely seized me, my legs found the speed to quickly tear me away from those dreary uninhabited buildings. Stopping at the other end of the fence to catch my breath, my eyes wandered toward the massive refrigerants of the *Centrale* looking for anyone climbing their long ladders attached to its side, but no humans were ever visible. With nothing else to investigate, I crossed the potato field to enter the school yard.

As school absences surpassed my number of days present, it was no surprise that the principal wished to confer with Mom. Surely it was not good news, nevertheless, the message was relayed. There was no urgency on Mom's part. After a few reminders from my teacher, one morning, Mom and baby Alfredo accompanied me to school.

Speaking in the school yard, the principal articulated the importance of attending school regularly. When it was all said and done, Elisa's new task was to ensure that I was ready for school before she left for hers. That arrangement suited me perfectly. Waking up in the darkness alone was eliminated, my fear remained my secret, and it allowed for a little more time with my sister.

From that day forward, attending school became routine, although, the best part of my day was still after school. For obvious reasons, my escapades in the pasture went undisclosed. Discretely climbing through the barbed wire fence left scratches on my arms and legs that were difficult to hide. Since my ventures were typically alone, it was never so far that the rooftop of our house was not in my view from the field. That haven filled endless hours among the butterflies, frolicking through millions of buttercups, poppies, daisies and dandelions that grew for as far as one could see. Lounged in a bed of grass as the sun soaked my soul, my mind pondered the universe. Is the sky made up of big blocks attached all together with massive heavy-duty nails to make sure it did not fall on top of us? What gave it its beautiful color? Was that why Pop had chosen a light blue mobylette?

When my mind was free of thoughts, a bouquet of wildflowers was picked for Mom, not thinking that the cow manure smeared on my shoes as well as where the flowers had come from would need some explanation. Needless to say, Mom was angry, threatening a *paliatone*[18] which implicated a wooden spoon. Every trip to the pasture exposed me a little more, but my legs could usually outrun my mother's when she chased me around the table with the wooden spoon.

On nice afternoons, Jeanine, a young girl from *Rue d'Eggaliere* picked me up to walk around the neighborhood or to chitchat with Mom and baby Alfredo Salvatore on the front steps. It was Mom's favorite spot to knit or hem dresses. On the Sundays when Jeanine had access to the family car, she offered me and Elisa a ride to the big church in *Hornaing, Saint Jean-Baptiste*. Otherwise, we walked to the *Chapel Heurteau* down the street. My parents joined us when the Italian priest served Mass at the chapel.

Children had their own seating area that was accessed through the side entrance. Church to me predominantly meant "singing." Not having a singing voice never deterred me. To make matters worse, my vocals were always exaggerated and stopping on queue when the hymn ended seemed really silly to me. A whisper in Elisa's ear by one of the monitors was her cue to escort me out of the church. Embarrassed and angry, she delivered her own sermon all the way home. Weaved in, were threats about not taking me to church ever again. Then, she revealed that my cooperation during the church service would be rewarded by a strawberry *boule*. With that, my choice was made!

Over time, we really enjoyed the ease of going to the market to buy what we needed. Accordingly, Pop removed our chicken coop and rabbit cubbies. The feces infested sand in the cubbies was all that was left to clean out. Since the animals had vacated their home, my friend and I designated it a perfect place to create one for ourselves. Requesting permission was moot, we knew

---

[18] Paliatone: Orsaresi word meaning being hit with many shovels or with one shovel many times.

better. Instead, we sneaked inside the lower cubby where we played all afternoon.

Climbing up the steps of our back porch after my friend left, red droplets began to trickle from my nose. Having dealt with bloody noses before, Mom dabbed a little vinegar on a handkerchief then held it lightly against my nose. My head tilted back offered a prefect view of mom's angry eyes as she yelled about the filth stuck in my hair. Clearly something that she didn't have to look too hard to notice. Blood that had started to drip from my ears and mouth provoked some gagging. In an instant, fear replaced her anger.

Mom bolted across the street to the Krawczyk's for aid. Nellie had a license and the family car was home, so she drove us to the hospital in *Somain*. The hemorrhage was cauterized, but observation and a surgical procedure planned for the following morning required an overnight stay. Naturally, Mom became hysterical after being told that she was not permitted to stay in the hospital with me. She was relentless.

In the end, they reluctantly released me for the night. The nurse provided Mom with the pre-operative instructions. Mom did not speak French. Neither the nurse nor Nellie spoke Italian. Hence, Mom had no idea what was wrong with me, she only understood her promise to return me to the hospital in the morning.

After a hearty breakfast, Mrs. Krawczyk drove us to the hospital. Pop took a day of leave to accompany us. He was not risking the loss of another child in the hospital. Pop's decent French facilitated communication. Upon our arrival, my parents proudly shared the details of my bountiful breakfast. The doctors were thoroughly displeased. What was clear was that the surgery could not wait without the risk of significant hearing loss. Under the circumstances, the only choice was to proceed without anesthesia.

My feet and arms were strapped to the operating table. Fear seized me when the doctor turned to face me wearing his surgical mask. In the midst of screaming and thrashing, two nurses struggled to immobilize me. A third sat on top of me with her knees nudged between my hips and the operating table. My squirming made it impossible to insert their long fine needles into my ears and nose, forcing the surgeon to appeal for more muscle.

Seeing Pop enter the room was a huge relief. Being the strongest person in the world, for sure, he had come to save me. His pale face touched mine, crying. Not wanting him to cry, gave me the strength to calm down.

Within a few weeks, life was normal again. Granted, missing a few more weeks of school was not too disappointing!

In June 1963, Elisa graduated from the *Lafargue School for Girls*. In celebration, the graduates were customarily gifted new bicycles that they rode together from house to house. At ours, we served them sodas and pastries. Elisa joined the pack on her old bicycle. She would unveil her new one when Pop returned. Although he had vowed never to set foot in *Orsara* again, a black laced telegram from his beloved sister, Concetta, changed his mind. Her husband had lost his battle to an illness induced by the fumes of the factory of Northern Italy where he had worked for a few years.

Pop helped his sister with the funeral arrangements of his dear friend. They had already left their apartment and moved into our house on *Via Tasso* a few years earlier when Zio Pellegrino had become too ill to work.

Soon after Pop's return, he and my mother were in the common room together until well past midnight. Mom was putting some final touches on a dress for a client while Pop was playing Solitaire which, for him, was far better than going to sleep alone. Pop broke his game to go to the toilet on the porch when he caught a whiff of smoke that was coming from the house next door. His feet hardly touched the ground. He flew to their front door and pounded.

His shouts awakened other neighbors who also ran in his direction to help. When their door finally opened, thick dark smoke billowed while red hot flames had overtaken the kitchen. The father, mother and their young daughter all exited uninjured. They spent their next few days sleeping on our green sofa bed while their home was being repaired.

The camaraderie and compassion within our little community had been extraordinary. We had discovered true friendships with a new type of family in *City Heurteau*. Accordingly, it was with deep chagrin that in the summer of 1963, my parents decided to move to *Fenain*. Pop had learned that a home situated closer to the mine had become available. The Bonzanini family who lived on our street had a brother who was vacating their home. That dwelling was more spacious and within walking distance to the mine of *Agache*.

4

The Nord: Fenain (Part 2)

The truck transporting our belongings and Mr. Krawczyk's car carrying us caravanned the fifteen minutes between *Hornaing* and *Fenain*. Stepping out of the car, an abrupt heaviness rushed to the pit of my stomach as my eyes rested on a massive black mountain behind a large metal gate at the end of our street. Pop was already in mid-sentence describing the layout of the mine with obvious pride as he demonstrated its proximity to where he worked.

Rue Taffin was a short thoroughfare bordered by nine identical red brick double homes. Two large living room windows overlooking the street made this spacious home even brighter. Our main entry on the side of the house faced the black mountain that Pop had told us was a pile of coal waste called a *terril*.[19] Our main living quarters consisted of the living room, kitchen and a small laundry room. Cold water ran in a tiny white porcelain sink in one corner of the laundry room. The rest of that space was shared by the washing machine, a huge coal stove and a table that we squeezed into another corner for our breakfasts and lunches.

Surprisingly, the windows in both bedrooms on the upper level brought in considerably more light, avoiding my early morning fears. The cellar stocked our precious coal. The prosciutto, cheese, honey and cooked wine garnished the small shelf in the basement stairwell.

A cemented surface adjoining the laundry room provided a fantastic play area. Mom, who was still handy with field tools, had cleared the yard of its tall wild grasses with a sickle the week prior to our move. Pop had already designed his vegetable garden in his mind. A small covered utility space that housed our tools and bikes connected to a dilapidated wooden shack. Inside it was a dark cramped space with a dingy wooden podium: our bathroom. Peering inside the

---

[19] *Terril*: (French); Man-made mound (heap-formed) with waste material, a by-product of coal mining.

hole in the center of the platform to inspect its depth, lasted only a brief moment. The stench was far worse than that of the pasture behind our house in *City Heurteau* but had none of its splendor.

One car belonging to our neighbor across the street regularly parked on the thoroughfare. Once per month, a huge mystery truck drove through then disappeared inside the metal gates. With children in nearly every house, our street easily turned into a huge playground allowing friendships to grow easily.

Even Alfredo, then two years old, ventured to play outdoors more frequently. He still didn't like to get dirty. Atop of his shorts or long pants, he always sported a shirt with a bowtie matching almost every dress Mom had ever sewn. Whether in solids, stripes or polka dots in whatever color, the little man liked to look good.

On Saturday afternoons, we joined the other children of our street at the front door of Mrs. Bonzanini, the only person on our street that we knew had a television. If the door was not already open, it would open a few minutes before everybody's favorite show began. Sometimes it was hard to see through our little crowd but we were all thrilled to be there. No one ever entered the room or spoke during the show. When it was over, we politely thanked her before returning to the street with our games of tag or whatever else amused us.

If alone, occasionally, I meandered to the metal gate at the end of the street, stretching my neck to get a glimpse of Pop. Although seeing him would have caused other problems since we were forbidden to be there at all. All the same, the only things visible were a closer view of the black mountain and the carts that slowly hauled coal waste up the narrow track to its peak.

We easily settled into our new neighborhood. Mom's French was decent, allowing her to arrange for our milk and bread deliveries herself. In the summertime, the aroma of the delicious chocolate croissant reached our noses even before the bread truck turned onto our street. The stop was directly in front of our house. When we were all patient and respectful of their service to the clients, the driver divided a chocolate croissant among all of the children. My first time accepting it, still uneasy, I quickly ran inside the house to tell Mom. Mortified that I may have asked for the bread, she sent me back with money to pay for it. The driver nodded "no" from afar and smiled at Mom who was watching from our gate.

Pop already knew most of the men in our neighborhood through his work at the mine. At least four of the families on our street were Italian so Pop introduced additional clients to *Piccolo*.

In keeping with the tradition of the Nord, we closed our shutters at sundown. On nice days, the shutter ritual was an excuse for the adults to meander here and there chitchatting with neighbors while the children took over the street for a few more hours. Elisa had made new friends: Sonia, Marie Laine and Michel.

48

Jean Pierre lived nearby. Michel and his family lived in Southern France but spent summers with their aunt on our street.

They rode bicycles together, listened to music on the radio or wrote the lyrics of their favorite songs using Sonia's typewriter. Sonia's mom often treated the group of teenagers to potato latkes, a Polish recipe made with grated potatoes mixed with eggs, a veil of flour and onions. They were fried and savored with a bit of sugar or jam by the fine young taste buds! Elisa spent a lot of time at Sonia's and told me stories about their square bathtub inside the house. It had a faucet with both hot and cold water. One person fit in it perfectly. Sonia and Elisa took turns bathing in it. Sometimes with bubbles!

Much to my disappointment, the tagalongs on the bicycle with Elisa and her friends had become a thing of the past. Nevertheless, our early to bed routine allowed me to get to know her friends. Pop worked hard so he tired early, but he still hated to go to sleep alone. Mom called him a big baby and accused him of fearing to miss something. We laughed but we all went to bed all the same, often as early as 7:30. Once asleep, he did not awaken easily. Elisa listened for his snores, then we quietly huddled together on our window sill to talk with our friends. If we were not outside, they knew to meet us under the window.

The strict rules at home remained unchanged: being respectful, no back-talk and "NO" meant "NO!" The others were even simpler: stay away from boys, and, of course, help Mom with the little ones and the house without being asked. Then, there was that one rule that gave me the most trouble: always ask for permission. The rules were almost always followed except when boys talked to Elisa or we ventured too far outside our permitted boundaries. She still bribed me with candy. The rules were the rules with no opportunity for explanations. Not wanting Elisa to get into trouble and despite all the silver on my molars, we were talking candy, so this arrangement suited me.

Over our first summer in *Fenain*, Mom had oddly gone missing one day. Except for the knitting shop or her weekly errands at the open market, she seldom left the house. Elisa told me that Mom would return soon but by dinner time, Pop was absent as well. That did not feel right, we always ate together. The next morning, still no parents. Elisa told me to stop asking questions, they will come home with a big surprise. Still, there was neither surprise nor sight of my parents and fear was setting in about ever seeing them again. After another day of craziness, Elisa took me for a long bicycle ride to at a large familiar building in *Somain*. The hospital!

Walking through the long hallway as inconspicuously as possible, we finally spotted Mom. Sitting upright in a bed smiling from ear to ear, her eyes stayed fixed on a glass wall lined by beautiful babies on the other side. Some were in tiny cribs while others were in incubators. They were so beautiful.

Thrilled, I begged Mom to take one home. Without hesitation, she pointed to the incubator directly in front of me and said, "Sure, how about that one, his name is Gino." Approval was quickly offered along with my endorsement for choosing the most beautiful baby. Their discharge from the hospital would be delayed by a few days since Gino had jaundice. Unsurprisingly, we were detected by a nurse who sternly reminded Mom that children were not permitted to visit. After exchanging a few winks with Mom, Elisa opened the window then we said our goodbyes.

Pointing out that we were walking in the wrong direction after exiting the hospital, Elisa, who was oddly counting windows, retorted with a curt shush. When we stopped, she helped me onto her shoulders stretching us to the window sill for a perfect view of Mom and the most beautiful baby brother in the world. My own questions went unanswered, my role was strictly volleying baby preparation through the window between my sister and Mom. Our abettor, Mom's roommate, was watching for inbound nurses.

The remainder of our first summer in *Fenain* stayed busy. Gino, the happiest little boy I had ever encountered, became everyone's baby. Alfredo and I often strolled him together in his carriage up and down our street. His baptism at Saint Andre concluded the summer. Zio Antimo and his wife Elena became his long-distance godparents.

Zio was known to me only by the picture of him and Pop in their last moments together at the docks of Naples so long ago. It was the only photo that hung on our walls, above the green sofa. Letters that came and went told us that Zio had left Venezuela to be closer to our nonni in America. Nonno planned to apply for his citizenship. His hope was for us to join them too. Pop either smiled or joked, "I already have my America." Beyond that, it was not a subject that we ever talked about.

The end of summer marked the start of a new school year. Elisa enrolled at Marie Curie School in *Somain* for fashion design and patternmaking. I was very apprehensive to enter a new school, *Ecole des Tilleuls*. No one from our street was in my class. The walk there was a bit longer. It included a path alongside the railroad track that came with strict orders never to cross it. For my final stretch, the delicious perfume emanating from the lime trees that lined its street always told me that my school was near.

My teacher was kind and read to us every day. My favorite story was *The Adventures of Nanou and Nanoche*. Students sat two by two on wooden benches. A small white porcelain well near the corner was filled with black ink for all our school writing. I was not fond of fountain pens, the ink was messy. It frequently resulted in a scolding for the mediocrity of our penmanship. We had homework every school day. Mom too. She always looked over my shoulder saying that it helped her to learn French.

My first school friend was Danila. She was tall with straight dark hair and dark eyes. We played during recess and usually walked home together. Sometimes, Pop picked me up after school with his mobylette. Danila and I squeezed on the back seat together for the ride to our house where we played for a bit. We were seldom allowed to visit friends, however, we were always encouraged to invite them to our home. Not understanding the reason for this seemingly unjust rule, an invitation from a classmate to play after school sounded fine to me. Her parents owned the bar across the street from the mine of *Agache* which was halfway home from school. Not seeking permission certainly simplified my life, besides only stopping to play for a bit would go unnoticed by my parents.

Losing track of time, however, posed a few challenges for me. The most significant, peering outside, was the fact that it had started to get dark. Afraid to leave, our games continued. Unfortunately, it was only getting darker which left me more and more frightened to leave. The bar closed at midnight, forcing me to leave. The consequences of my tardiness was a scant passing thought while I ran all the way home as if something was chasing me.

The profound relief of arriving home quickly transformed into anxiety. Even in the darkness, Mom's distraught face against the glass pane of our back door was unmistakable. Pop, Elisa and neighbors were out searching for me. Overtaken by fear and running fast, I had not seen any of them in my path. Pop and Elisa walked through the door soon after to check in and there I was.

Everyone was upset but Mom was mega angry. Elisa immediately jumped between us when Mom grabbed my hair. Pop, who had not yet spoken, softly and firmly sent everyone to bed. Not rocking any more boats in one day, I made my usual rounds of good night kisses and quietly headed up the stairs. The following morning arrived with a recap of my after school responsibilities. Any misunderstanding on my part included the promise of a *paliatone*, implicating the dreaded wooden spoon. Threats were not necessary, I didn't want to see my family upset anymore or be out in the dark alone.

With the rhythm of the seasons, the holidays approached. We celebrated Christmas with the Luongo family in *Escaudain*. Mr. Luongo worked with Pop, and Mom met his wife in her seamstress world. Both families spoke Italian. They had three children: two daughters and a son close to Elisa's age. On Christmas Eve, all the girls gathered in a warm bedroom with a soft carpet.

Our collective eyes were glued to the window as we watched the snow flurries cover the town white. A magical end to an already perfect day. The window stayed open until we were all shivering. After our snowball battles in the morning, we gathered the purest of snow, drizzled some cooked wine on top, then feasted on our homemade popsicles. This was the first best Christmas of my life.

In turn, we hosted the Luongo's for the year-end holidays. Mamouch, our adopted "grandmother," who also spoke Italian with my parents, lived next door. She took care of her grand-daughter, Graziella, after school and during the summers so we spent a lot of time together. Since Mamouch was spending the holidays with her daughter, she left her house key for us and our guests.

Our holidays were not over until the *Befana* arrived. In the Nord, we did not hang stockings so she always hid a gift for us to find. On Epiphany, Gino and Alfredo found their gift in plain sight. The only thing tagged with my name was a heaping pail of coal.

That search for me was worth an entire bucket of bad. When my eyes filled with tears, Elisa told me to look harder but it was useless. There was nothing else. After hours of torture, Pop suggested abandoning my search in the low spots, perhaps it was time to look to higher ground. The six-piece red china set hung on a wall in the kitchen instantly came into view. I did not care so much about what my gift was, on the other hand, I cared deeply about that load of coal that I had earned. Clearly, the *Befana* was not happy about my nocturnal escapade at the bar either so I decided to be better.

Letters followed one another almost every day from Italy or America. Nonno always told us that America was a wonderful country with a thousand opportunities. He had obtained his American citizenship which would allow him to call us under a recent program that helped to reunify scattered families. Nonno added that he was going to start the formalities. Pop was not at all interested. His responses never wavered from, "We are very happy in the Nord. Our little family is together, we are peaceful, comfortable and we don't need anything else." Or, "I don't need to leave, I have my America here. We have our America in the Nord."

Then, Nonno Alfredo's accident happened and perspectives quickly began to shift. He had fallen off of a ladder while pruning a tree. Everyone was worried for the obvious reasons and also because our nonni could not survive in America without work for too long. Pop wired money to his parents over the next few months as Nonno underwent additional surgical procedures. It was becoming more unlikely that he would be able to work again. They wanted us to come to America, instead, Pop wired more money as their medical bills continued to mount.

In time, Pop arranged an appointment with Mr. Gernez, who owned the general store around the corner on the main street, to telephone his parents. Following that call, my parents were extremely distressed. They told us that our grandparents needed us but they did not expand on the details. Terrified that I already knew what it meant, my questions remained unasked.

As the summer days approached, the *ducasse* returned. The bumper cars were my favorite although I was very small and clumsy. Being stuck in a corner inside a pulsating car never deterred me. Around the same time, an annual ceremony for school awards, for which I had absolutely no interest in, also took place. Incapable of persuading Pop to leave me with my sister on the bumper cars, I sat quietly beside him during the ceremony. Hearing the mayor call my name over the microphone startled me. Not knowing what to do, Pop nudged me forward. With knees shaking, I made my way onto the stage to accept my award of two books for being first in my class. That surprise that also came with a very proud look on Pop's face was beyond delightful. Wanting to enjoy that look again for as long as possible, I decided to work really hard in school.

Being a little older came with additional summer responsibilities. Looking after Gino or Alfredo was not easy. Neither could be left alone even for a moment. Gino was curious about everything. He climbed the china cabinet but could not descend. Alfredo loved taking things apart to see how they worked. Screwdrivers were hidden but he always found them. My brother even tested electrical outlets that he fortunately survived without injury! He fixed one of Pop's watches that had not worked in years with a few parts left over.

When there was absolutely nothing left to do, we sat together on the stoop of our front door to count the trips that the carts made up and down the black mountain to discard coal waste. We waved to Pop from time to time, pretending that he saw us. Alfredo asked me if it was Pop's job to make the mountain taller. Unaware of what Pop did at the mine, I simply said, "Yes, of course."

Knowing my way around the neighborhood allowed me to assist with some errands. On Thursdays, Mom sent me to the butcher. Taking my usual spot on the little platform near the counter for the butcher to easily find me, I patiently waited for my turn. He always smiled and offered me a ring of sausage.

For incidentals, Mom sent me to Gernez. During my first visit in the store alone, I took my time exploring. The building was huge from the outside but the store itself did not appear to be particularly big. Every corner was packed with a little bit of everything: vegetables, pasta, plus all sorts of gadgets that I did not recognize. A small rack near the counter filled with school supplies caught my eye. Mr. Gernez walked beside me to offer his assistance. Realizing my dilly-dallying for too long, my focus returned to what Mom needed and left.

Running errands allowed me to keep the change, if it was coins. After collecting enough to purchase a notebook and a pen, I returned to Gernez. In that notebook, I was free to write whatever my heart desired. Furthermore, penmanship didn't count, although, it was practiced anyway. The school rules were very strict. It was not uncommon for the teacher to crumple an assignment. Then, the catastrophe was tucked in the collar on the back of the neck for display during recess. I loved going to school but making mistakes really frightened me.

Second grade was the first year that boys and girls were separated in our school. The classrooms for the boys were on the left side of the building while those for the girls were on the right. A fence separated us in the schoolyard in the event teachers were unsuccessful in policing the co-mingling. The fragrant lime trees sprinkled in the courtyard masked the odor from the bathroom stalls on the far end.

Uniforms were not required, instead we wore smocks. Mom was not particularly fond of the dull colors and styles found in the stores so she sewed ours in colorful fabrics. On the first day of school, lined up to enter the building, my teacher stopped me. You never wanted to be stopped in line. Having already expressed my concern to Mom that it looked like a dress, my hands quickly lifted its hemline to reveal my actual dress underneath. The teacher's demeanor immediately changed. She expressed her delight in the choice of vivid colors. Even so, I begged Mom to shorten it just a bit so that my dress showed below.

My favorite subjects were math and reading. Memorizing recitations and speaking in front of the class made me nervous. For that reason, I practiced the poem *Au Paysage d'Octobre* to the point that Mom and Alfredo also knew it by heart. Alfredo was missing his front teeth and needed to wipe saliva that dribbled from the side of his mouth after each line. He always knew when he messed up and it was comical to hear him restart each and every time.

Our teachers were nice but strict. Talking in class was punishable by a time-out behind one of the two freestanding blackboards. We stood to respond to questions. Occasionally, correct answers were rewarded with colorful animated cards called *les images* that we accepted with great pride. The cards depicted animals, fruits and places that we had never seen before with facts about their origin. Our exams, at the end of each quarter, resulted in new seating assignments. The students were arranged on the benches from highest to lowest marks. There was no privacy when it came to grades. A perk for being in the front bench was the close proximity to the enormous coal furnace in the center of the classroom.

With my heart set on new books at the end of the school year, it was necessary to persuade Mom to let me stay for *Les Etudes*, a paid afterschool enrichment program. She had noted that it was already taking me too long to return home afterschool. Elisa arrived later from her school in *Somain* so Mom needed me to look after my brothers while she prepared dinner. My dilemma was to figure out how to do both. I really didn't want to give up the first chair.

The next day, chats with my friends after school were abandoned in place of running all the way home as fast as my legs could carry me. No one seemed to notice my effort so over dinner, I boastfully broadcast my triumph in the race from school. They wanted to know who else was involved in this race. How far was it? Genuinely annoyed with all the irrelevant questions on the subject, I stood my ground. "I raced alone, won alone and got home early. The end!" With that, Mom gave me the dues to enroll in *Les Etudes*. When the school year ended, with knees shaking, again, I proudly accepted my treasured books at the summer awards ceremony.

That summer was full of surprises and discoveries. Pop had built a new wooden gate that he painted in his favorite color, light blue. This one locked to keep our very sociable Gino from escaping. The key hung above the gate at easy reach for our friends and neighbors. There was nothing that discouraged the always smart and unpredictable Gino. He often climbed over it, although he was occasionally left dangling from the top boards. Steadfast, he patiently waited until a passerby rescued him. Neighbors usually honored his desire to be in his favorite place, street side, where they played with him for a bit then placed him back into our yard.

On some days consumed by boredom, I waited at the corner to wave to the summer camp children when they passed all together down the main road. Among them were my friends from our street. I wished to be with them but my parents said camp was not necessary. Instead, I played ball, jumped rope, had fun with my brothers and helped Mom. It was during those dull and annoying chores that some of my best discovery were made. While picking up a few diapers that had fallen on the bedroom floor, stacks of magazines under my parents' bed captured my attention. They were all written in Italian. Mom and Pop spoke to us in Italian, but we responded in French. How hard could it be to read them?

After bringing the diapers to Mom, my attention quickly returned to my forbidden treasure. The *Bolero* magazines included weekly recurring stories. After placing them in chronological order, the story about the adventures of a character named Elize easily flowed. It was all written in photo frames similar to comic books. It wasn't difficult to get the gist of the story. Quickly getting hooked on that storyline about a women doing amazing things, kept me vigilant for the follow-on editions.

That summer also brought furry additions to our family. The first was a grey cat that we found in our utility area. Over the course of the week, I named that friendly and cuddly guy Nanou, then I "accidentally" let him inside the house to spend the night. My parents were beyond peeved to see him the following morning. It didn't take much persuasion to allow Nanou to stay after that. We had no idea where he spent his days, but he always returned at night to curl up behind the small coal stove in our living room.

The other furry guy named Yukie, was charged with protecting our house. Yukie was a handsome and very loud medium size dog with a gold and rust coat. He stayed in our yard in a large wooden house that Pop had built and painted for him. Yukie ate what we ate, and I was certain that he was Italian by his refusal to eat pasta until it was appropriately presented with tomato sauce and grated cheese. A meatball on top made it simply divine.

On the flipside, we collectively experienced a deeply traumatic event with the cave-in that occurred at the mine of *Agache*. One day, Pop did not return home after his shift. It was completely out of character for him to be hours late without any word. Mom was naturally very upset. Accompanied by other wives from our neighborhood in the same predicament, they marched together to the mine where they learned that there had been a cave-in earlier in the day and their husbands were trapped in a gallery.

Several more hours of anguish passed before they finally made contact with some of the trapped workers and information came to light about the size of the situation. Over the next few hours, one by one, they were freed from their deep prison. The workers were given the option to ascend individually by cage but they all refused. In solidarity, they ascended all together around midnight after they were all freed. As each worker was liberated from the cage when they reached the earth, Mom recognized Pop only by his tired and shaken eyes.

This was the first time that Mom had seen her husband at his job completely covered in coal dust. She was terrified. It was then, that realization had set in that my father spent his days two thousand feet underground. Although I still did not fully grasp what he did, it was clear that it had nothing to do with transporting coal waste to the top of the black mountain. We were all infinitely shaken by the harsh reality of Pop's daily life. It also incited more parental discourse that, over time, tilted the pendulum toward going to America.

As the summer of 1964 closed, so did Elisa's window to begin the second year in her program of studies at Marie Curie. She had spent several months caring for all of us while Mom recuperated from an operation. Instead, she joined the Academy of Lille in a cooperative program alternating between classes in fashion design and working in their thread mill. She took the bus before I awakened and returned just before dinner which made her time at home even scarcer.

Mom stayed busy as a seamstress. She also learned to crochet. Scavenging her leftover yarn, allowed me to practice various stitches that resulted in many patches of nothing. From time to time, I accompanied her to the yarn shop where the vendor always took the time to teach Mom new stitches. She added those samples to her collection for beautiful new hats, scarves and gloves that kept us warm throughout the winter. In an outing at Danila's home, I observed that her mom owned a knitting machine. After mentioning it to Mom, they worked out a sewing for knitting exchange since Danila's mother did not sew.

Winters in the Nord were wet and bitter cold. On those Sunday afternoons, we gathered in the living room, the warmest room in the house, near the coal stove. My parents spent endless hours playing Italian card games of scopa and briscola over many conversations. Pop was a sore loser, always trying to make some sort of deal with Mom. It was hilarious to hear their discourse when she won multiple games in a row. He simply charmed her into changing the rules then they broke into laughter. The rest of us were in the vicinity doing this or that. I played and discreetly listened to their stories about America, life and our family.

Some things I understood, others not so much. Zio Antimo was urging us to go to America. He said it was a better life. Pop did not want to go and didn't want to think about it. He said everything here was peaceful, we were fine and everything we needed was already in France. Mom, who was still shaken by the mine accident, encouraged him to consider it more seriously. What was very clear, was that they both worried about Nonno. With their last hand of cards, they both agreed to decide another day.

Much to Alfredo's disappointment, he began kindergarten in the fall 1965. He had no interest in leaving home and Mom saw no reason to wake him up early. When he awakened each morning, he cleverly asked what day it was. On Thursday or Sunday, he expressed a seemingly genuine desire to go to school. We did not have school on those days. In the event that he did wake up on time, Mom accompanied us to school, along with Gino, who observed a new world from his carriage. Without fail, Alfredo was either thirsty or hungry as soon as we arrived at the schoolyard. Mom, incapable of leaving a hungry child, took him home.

That frustrating habit was cured in one day when Elisa walked us to school. As expected, Alfredo arrived thirsty. I was incredulous when Elisa pulled out a water bottle that she had hidden in Gino's baby carriage. He took a few sips then Elisa urged him to go into the schoolyard with me. Alfredo acknowledged that he would like to but couldn't because he was famished. She cleverly pulled a sandwich with butter and strawberry jam from the same place. Looking a bit crushed, he took a few nibbles then he let me take his hand to lead him into the schoolyard.

My classroom was occupied by two grades which allowed me to enter the third grade with the same teacher, Mrs. Rudant. That year I made another special friend, Nadine. She had light brown hair that rested on her shoulders, bangs, and always wore a wide white headband. Being exceptionally bright, she had skipped second grade and we occupied the first bench together for the remainder of the school year.

She, Danila and I remained close friends and stayed for *Les Etudes*, then we walked home all together. Since my house was on the way to theirs, they often stopped to play for a bit before they walked the rest of the way together.

That year, Mrs. Rudant's husband died. During her absence, the students in our class were dispersed across the other grades for several weeks. A few of us were a bit intimidated to be placed with the fifth graders because it was taught by the principal. Our benches were too heavy and big to move. After filling their empty seats, we squeezed in here and there seated on upside down wastebaskets and shared tight workspaces. We had our own work to do but the teacher invited us to do the same work as the fifth graders.

In preparation for Mrs. Rudant's return, a few of us volunteered to tidy up the classroom. The principal also requested that we deliver some papers to her home. I had no idea where she lived but my classmate did. It was across the railroad tracks situated on the other side of our school, but an underpass removed the crossing danger.

The narrow passage was dark, dirty and full of graffiti but on the other side was a *Fenain* that I had never known existed. Momentarily frozen, that unexpected magnificent view of homes and gardens that were all attractively manicured all around was drawn in. Even the streets had a different look with a warmer texture. When we knocked on her door, Mrs. Rudant opened it onto lovely furniture of interesting styles. My shoes came off at the front door as my feet sank into a very plush carpet. Incredibly amazed by this different *Fenain*, just for a moment, I wondered if other places like it existed.

At home, my *Bolero*, enthusiastically awaited, was read stretched out on the floor of my parents' bedroom incognito. While eavesdropping during one of their card games, Mom mentioned to Pop that the subsequent issue of the magazine had arrived. Pop, in turn, asked if Elize had survived her ordeal. Since it was a hot topic for me as well, I had already read it and the words that she had survived slipped out much too quickly. Stunned, Pop asked how I knew. The heat that flushed my face told them all that they needed to know.

The feeling of being spared when they both fell silent was replaced with profound regret the following week when the space underneath their bed was barren of *Bolero* magazines.

Over the course of the summer, talks of going to America became more serious. Pop had taken multiple trips to Paris. A final notice for submitting necessary papers to the embassy left my parents deeply puzzled. They had always responded to all of their requests. They scrambled to collect and send all of the necessary documents by the deadline. The truth was discovered many years later. Elisa and Pop were usually the first ones up to start the fire. Although Elisa was happy to be rejoining our extended family in America, she did not want another new start. I had seen her and Michel hand-in-hand. As for Sonia, Marie Laine and Jean Pierre, she would miss them immensely. She had decided to intercept the notices and burned them in the coal stove. Elisa was torn but when the final notice arrived, she felt guilty.

Things progressed very quickly over the next month. Pop arranged for a car with our neighbor to travel to the American Embassy in Paris for our physicals and other required formalities. My excitement about this journey to Paris quickly dissolved upon realizing that my place was next to Alfredo in the open trunk area behind the back seat. He suffered from motion sickness. That day was no different, he vomited a few miles into the trip. Mom handed me a cloth diaper that we brought in anticipation to clean it up, then she pulled him up to sit on her lap. Gino was already on Elisa's lap. The smell was so nauseating, it soaked into the foam pad that had been placed there to make us more comfortable. It did not take long before I vomited too, but there was no place for me to go. More cloth diapers came in my direction which were stacked on top of the others. The windows were opened while I stayed motionless for the rest of the trip to keep from getting sick again.

We arrived at the American Embassy at the crack of dawn because, for Pop, on time meant we were late. When the building opened, we were first in line. The entire morning was spent amid obligatory lung x-rays, vaccinations and tons of papers to fill out. We were informed that they needed a bit of time to audit all the documents before approving the visas. We could receive our results by mail or return to the embassy after lunch.

We were not leaving without our visas and, with the exception of Pop, it was our first time in Paris. We seized the opportunity to see the Arc of Triumph and the Eiffel Tower which, admittedly, I had always imagined as golden. Then we strolled along the Seine River. On this special day, Pop treated us and our driver to lunch at a restaurant where we could choose anything we wanted from the menu. I had never been to a restaurant. The prepared platters on display were irresistible, especially the one heaping with French fries. Elisa told me French fries were not a lunch and accentuated the reality that I could never finish it. Although my choice was firm, as usual, she was right!

When we returned to the embassy after lunch, our collective joy turned into incredible chaos and confusion in only an instant. We received only five visas! A dark spot on Mom's x-ray precluded her approval to enter the USA. We were all crying as Pop tried to calmly explain that the spot was not cancer. Two ribs had been removed to access a benign cyst on her lung while she was still living in Italy. His voice remained steady and on point, but I could tell he wanted to scream. It was hopeless. Without medical proof, the embassy would not validate her passport. It was a very dark journey back to *Fenain*.

The following weeks were traumatic as Mom and Pop considered various alternatives. They knew that collecting the papers needed from Italy could take a long time. They determined that the children would go to America as planned with Pop while Mom would return to Italy temporarily. They felt that obtaining a visa from Italy to America would be easier for her.

I could sense that not even Pop was satisfied with that option, but no one asked questions in the hopes that it would not become a reality. To everyone's relief, Mom's visa arrived unexpectedly about a month later. Our community physician, Dr. De la Robertie, had written a letter to the American Embassy that sufficiently satisfied their concerns. The idea of our family being separated no longer terrified me. Instead, I was completely consumed by intense fear of leaving France, the only home that I knew.

My parents sent a telegram to our nonni in America that we had good news to share and confirmed an appointment with Mr. Gernez to use the telephone. This was a special call so we went as a family. My brothers and I were particularly excited, we had never seen a telephone. As it turned out, that was not the only revelation. Their home was absolutely stunning. It was hard for me to imagine that such splendidness existed behind the walls of the cluttered store. A glass door led into an equally beautiful tiled floor with a built-in dark wooden bench against each wall. It seemed that the telephone had its own room! Mr. Gernez initiated the call with the operator. Once a connection was made, he turned the handset over to Pop then swiftly disappeared to offer us privacy.

Pop confirmed our good news with his parents, then we all took turns to say a few words on the telephone. Nonno told me that I will be speaking English soon and proceeded to give me my first lesson on the telephone by counting from one to ten. Many things finally registered with me that day. I fully grasped the reality that they did not speak French. The real shocker was hearing Pop tell his parents that we would arrive in America by Christmas. Less than three months away! It had taken two years to complete all the paperwork, I didn't expect that actually leaving would be so quickly. In fact, I didn't really expect to leave at all. I was worried about school in America and the heaviness in my stomach returned. Anxious for some fresh air, I was relieved to see Mr. Gernez promptly reappear when we finished. A call to the operator confirmed our charges and we left.

The subsequent month was extraordinarily busy. There were countless deliberations around what to bring with us, what to sell and what to give away. My parents made it look easy but every aspect of it seemed complicated to me.

I was immensely worried and upset. Pop had purchased a large metal crate to ship a few items: sewing machine, linens, Mom's American silk dress and the rose silk bedspread. Given the limited space, I was offered the choice of two books to take with me. I didn't have many but wanted to retain my school awards, so I hid a third, *Tale of the illuminated island* by Bouliaguet in the trunk.

The next school year began regardless of our plans which added even more distress in overhearing that our airline tickets had been purchased. Our departure date was set for November 5, 1966. Still, it did not feel real and I had no idea of exactly how to convey it to Mrs. Longelin, my fourth grade teacher. So, I didn't. Pretending everything was normal, I continued going to *Les Etudes* after school, just in case.

Around that time, some of my friends were preparing for their sacrament of First Holy Communion. Now older and allowed to cross the railroad tracks, Alfredo and I faithfully went to the Saint Andre church together. After Mass, I asked the priest for permission to join catechism. When he looked for a parent, I confessed that my parents were not there but they would approve. I hoped! Hand-in-hand Alfredo and I walked home with my new Missal. I was relieved when Pop wrote my name in it…perhaps it meant that we would not leave.

Everyone told me, "You must be happy to go to America." My uncertainty felt guilty and my biggest worries changed by the day. Among those distresses were Yukie, Nanou and Nanoche, another cat that I had convinced my parents needed a home. Pop said our friends would take care of them, but my questions about "who" and "where," found no answers. In the end, it did not matter since those needs changed quickly too. Yukie occasionally escaped on adventures but, never one to miss a meal, he always returned by dinner time. One day, he returned long after dinner bloodied and limping. Pop helped him into a box with a blanket to make him comfortable in our utility room. When Pop told us his injuries were serious, my brothers and I sobbed so he sent us all to bed. Pop was not fond of dogs, but that evening we clearly saw the deep sadness in his eyes. Throughout the night, Pop never left his side. By morning, Yukie was gone. A few days later, Nanoche did not return home either. The word on the street was that she had been seen on the main road. Perhaps our furry friends also knew that we were leaving. My entire world was already changing too fast. Confessing my fears about Nanou being left alone, my friend Grazielle and Mamouch promised me that they would take care of my cat.

November arrived far too soon. There were final dinners, gatherings and a continuous line of friends at our door with offers of best wishes. Some took photos of us with the children on our street. Since Alfredo had become a street friend too, including him in the photos was important to me, but he was always so stubborn. I promised to hold his hand and bring him back inside the house as soon as we finished. His grip was beyond tight that I did not dare let go as promised, otherwise, for sure he would never trust me again. Our last Thursday in France was reserved for a dinner with Elisa's friends and mine. That night, we ate pasta, salad and Mom's special lemon tarts for dessert.

With days left, procrastinating the inevitable was futile. Struggling to find my voice, the words finally cracked into a confession to my teacher that it was my last week of school in France. After school on that Friday I hugged my friends in the hallway, collected my coat, and then sought out my teacher to pay my dues for *Les Etudes*. Already walking in my direction, Mrs. Longelin pulled me into her arms and said, "Keep it. Have a beautiful life in America. When you get there, buy something nice for yourself with it and think of me." We both cried. I loved this school to which I would never return.

That Friday was also the last day in our home. We were expected to vacate by midnight so it could be readied for its next occupant. By early evening, our beds, tables and sofa were moving across and down our street. Even the stove was going to our neighbor across the street. Ours was in much better condition so the men swapped them. We ate dinner at the home of Mamouch. Then, we gathered with friends and neighbors at the church where the priest performed a special blessing for us. That night we slept on our own mattresses spread on Mamouch's living room floor. They were already promised but would be picked up by neighbors after we left in the morning.

At five o'clock Saturday morning, we filled our neighbor's trunk with the suitcases for our journey to the airport in Paris. Before climbing into the car, I observed our neighbors all lined up along our street. Some were waving, others threw air kisses, and most of them were crying. That heaviness in my stomach returned along with all sorts of other thoughts fluttering through my mind. Hearing my parents say that we could not travel to Italy each year, no doubt, we would not return to France either. They said, we will have a better life in America but I liked my life here. I liked my friends, I liked my school and I liked our home. I still did not like the dark but I was sure it would get dark in America too.

We piled into the car. Sonia wanted to accompany my sister to the airport so her mother drove a second car. Seeing the back of Elisa and Sonia's heads in the car in front of ours assured me that Elisa was really coming with us. That was the moment that in my heart I knew my life was over. My home was no longer my home. I turned around to look through the rear window of the car one last time until we turned the corner. Then, as if someone just turned out the lights, my world completely disappeared.

5

America

Pop's schedule followed to the letter, placed our arrival at the Paris Orly Airport with more than plenty of time to spare. We rapidly freed ourselves of the six supersized suitcases at the check-in counter. Taking full advantage of the one per person limit, each was filled to the brim with our important documents, some photos and our best clothes. Every nook and cranny was jam-packed with our immediate necessities like the espresso coffee pot and our jumbo silverware that my sister and I had hoped to abandon.

Elisa and Sonia were huddled in a corner, as private as one could find in a busy airport, embracing their final moments together. My brothers and I, tired, excited and anxious of what lay ahead, had taken over a bench nearby. All three of us sported matching white cardigan sweaters with tiny sparkly specks of red, blue, green and gold. Danila's mom had knitted them by machine. Their delivery had provided a perfect excuse to spend more time with Danila during our final days.

Gino and Alfredo were twins in their matching grey plaid double breasted coats, white shirts and navy blue bowties. Mom had sewn new outfits for everyone except for the new suit that Pop had purchased for this special adventure. My white dress had green pleats just below the hipline. Green zigzag piping bordered the neckline. For Elisa, she had sewn a grey pencil skirt topped with a beautiful silver sweater that was purchased from a small boutique in *Somain*. We each had a brand new coat and a new pair of shoes even though our old ones were not worn.

A powerful feeling overcame us all with the call for our flight. After seeing Elisa and Sonia hug another one last time, we solemnly followed our pre-drilled protocol to always hold a hand. Skeptical to believe Pop who had a tendency to embellish his stories, the Boeing 707 really was as big as a house. Our seats were easily found since our family occupied the entire last row of the airplane.

Mom, Pop and Gino filled one side. Alfredo vomited in the aisle prior to reaching our seats on the other side of aisle. Bile odor relief arrived when Mom decided to keep an eye on him, so we traded Alfredo for Gino.

As the plane lifted over the clouds, a spectacular view of the Eiffel Tower and the Arc of Triumph emerged. It intensified the excitement for the next part of our adventure. Knowing Elisa remembered our family from *Orsara*, millions of questions were on the tip of my tongue. However, the grief plainly visible on her face was cue enough to abandon the interrogation and let her pretend to sleep. On the other side of the aisle, Pop's snoring prompted Alfredo to dash over to our side where we watched a movie on the big screen at the front of the plane together. The opportunity to watch a film was another unexpected and amazing surprise. Over the six hour flight, drifting in and out of sleep helped to calm our excitement and lessen our worries.

Our arrival in New York was beyond overwhelming. My brothers and I were stunned by the massive crowds everywhere we turned at the JFK Airport. Everyone immediately sought their designated hand. Pop tirelessly filled out papers.

By the time we crept up to the front of the line in customs where our first suitcase was opened, a perfect view of the upper level appeared. Above us, on our right, a glass wall separated all of the relatives and friends who waited for the passengers in customs. They were so tightly packed that one would think it impossible to find their loved ones, but everyone did. An elevated air of excitement was created all around us when Elisa spotted Zio Antimo. Pop's eyes welled as he pointed out each family member to me and my brothers who did not know that part of the family.

Nonno was easy to pinpoint on his crutches, making the others easier to locate. Suddenly, the entire world around our family faded. Feeling our energy, the customs clerk smiled, stopped asking questions and never opened the other five suitcases. Racing to join our family on the other side of the glass, we found the whole world had come to welcome us: our nonni, Zio Antimo, Zia Elena and their son Alfredo Mario who was the same age as Gino. Even Nonno's sister, Zia Emilia who had emigrated in her teens so many years ago, was in the midst with her daughter and son-in-law.

It was dark outside and bitter cold when we exited the airport. We were all tired and jet-lagged facing another few hours by car to reach our final destination in Bethlehem, Pennsylvania. Everyone familiar to me piled in Zio's car. When space ran out, I was volunteered to ride in the car with Zia Emilia's family and our nonni. They seemed really nice, nevertheless, it troubled me to be separated not only from my sister but my little brothers too. Sitting between Nonna and Zia in the back seat, my neck stretched to keep an eye on Zio's white Chevrolet station wagon directly in front of us. With millions of cars crossing the bridge in New York in the dark, it was an impossible task. Zia Emelia astutely assessing my distress, assured me that Zio Antimo knew the way. Resting my head on her lap while Nonna pulled my feet onto hers, Zia gently stroked my hair as my tired eyes fought to stay awake and listen to their chats.

Around two in the morning, our car arrived in Fountain Hill, a small borough of Bethlehem. My worried look alerted Zia Emilia to quickly re-affirm that the rest of my family was not far behind.

From the street, the house appeared pitch black. It occurred to me that with the entire world at the airport to welcome us, there was no one at home to keep the fire going. Every part of me wanted to stay in the warmth of the car. That distress melted when the gentle heat enveloped me as quickly as Nonna unlocked the door. When the light switch was flicked on, there was no sign of a coal stove or fireplace. In that magical moment, I admitted that, yes, perhaps life could be better in America!

Nonni lived on the main floor of their two-story brick home. An identical second floor was reserved for us to rent. Each level included a kitchen, living room, one bedroom and an indoor bathroom with a real bathtub.

As promised, and to my great relief, the other car arrived minutes later. The children all slept on the mattresses spread on the floor upstairs that my parents had pre-paid for our arrival: one matrimonial and four twin mattresses. Elisa was thrilled over the separate beds. Something to do with complaints about kicking in my sleep. Nonetheless, that night, we all fell asleep quickly and stayed very warm!

While we lived on the second floor, we only went upstairs to sleep or bathe. Our mattresses were scattered over those three rooms. Dinners were shared downstairs with the entire extended family and were very festive. Nonno strategically occupied his spot at the kitchen table where he could easily get in and out with his crutch always within reach. Being very independent, he had learned to walk with one crutch to free his other arm. His right shoe was also augmented with a heel of about two inches. Nonno was an older version of Pop and just as jovial.

During our first few weeks in America, a bottle of Four Roses Whiskey alongside the bottles of homemade wine and Ballantine beer took permanent residence on the table. Day after day, Mom and Pop reacquainted with *Orsaresi* friends while making new ones. The friendly encounters also highlighted the quandary for me and my brothers that no one spoke French. We heard only English and *Orsaresi*. We understood the dialect but always responded in French. Our nonni were very vocal about their displeasure with our communication with them, or lack thereof. We were not happy either.

The routine of everyday life soon took over. Nonna rode the bus to a garment factory in the city of Allentown before we awakened each morning and returned at dinner time. She had begun that job after Nonno's accident. Nonno babysat for our cousin Alfredo Mario during the day as his parents both worked. Obviously, every offspring had an Alfredo namesake in honor of Nonno. To distinguish between the Alfredos, we often gave them a nickname or called them by their middle name. Our logic worked for us.

Pop and Elisa began working a week after we arrived. Pop's visa included a work permit as a general worker for a steel fabrication company called Bethlehem Fabricators where his brother was also employed. They primarily constructed car carriers sourced from the local Bethlehem Steel Company. Zio had explained that welders were paid more. Accordingly, Pop decided to learn that skill. Over the next few weekends, he and his brother drove to a shop owned by Zia Emilia's son in New Jersey. He had recently set up his own small welding business. While they assisted her son in the shop, Pop learned to weld. Soon after, he moved to a better paying welder position.

Elisa worked in a dress factory with Zia Elena. After my aunt dropped off her son at nonni's, the pair walked the few blocks together to the factory. Mom took care of things at home and prepared dinner for all of the workers. Night after night was filled with catching up, then everyone went home and it all repeated the next day.

As for me, anxiety heightened surveying my new school that was situated directly across the street. The kitchen window offered a perfect view of the two playgrounds positioned on either side of the brick building. Oddly, each was co-mingled with boys and girls who appeared to be permitted to play together.

Nonno had unsuccessfully tried to register me and Alfredo. We still needed to show proof of residency and vaccination records. As hard as my grandparents tried, it became apparent in our first days that they really struggled with the English communication too.

When Zia Elena accompanied us a few days later, we learned that part of the difficulty in getting us registered was the school's inability to handle foreign students. They placed Alfredo in kindergarten so it would be easier for him to learn the language. Being older, I posed a bigger challenge for the school. They needed time to make special arrangements with a different school. When Zia stressed the need for me begin as quickly as possible, they reluctantly agreed to have me sit in their fourth grade classroom while the necessary preparations were made. It was profoundly troubling that they did not know what to do with me and that special programs were even necessary!

My fourth grade classroom resembled nothing that I could have even imagined. No large coal furnace commanded the center the classroom, yet the entire room was heated. Similar to the playground, the classroom was co-educational and each student occupied an individual desk. The seemingly kind teacher greeted me, then escorted me to an empty desk at the front of the classroom. Undeniably, it was not at all disappointing to learn that seat placement was not tied to academic achievement.

The students were nice and easily included me in their playground games of four-square and Chinese jump rope. The classroom was much more relaxed than I had been accustomed to. Neither uniforms nor smocks were required. Perhaps, it was because we did not have to stress over ink wells or fountain pens.

Instead of students lining up at the school entrance with the teacher's whistle, we were expected to be in our seats before the morning bell. Each morning and after recess, a crowd of students typically gathered around my desk to talk. Them in English, me in French. There were no expectations for me to complete any school assignment. Every day, all day long, I sat, listened and mostly daydreamed about how I wished that scenario to be.

Despite having fully expected school to be difficult, it felt painfully impossible. My eyes scanned the books that crowded the shelves on the back wall of the classroom. Even the thought of wishing to read them seemed hopeless.

A few weeks of no homework seemed to really upset Zio Antimo. One evening, he lost it while I, completely discouraged and beyond ashamed, simply sobbed. The following day, with great difficulty and even greater determination, I requested a book to start learning English. My teacher's impression fueled my sentiment that she did not trust any book setting on that shelf would help me, but we settled on one anyway. She was right. Disheartened, I simply gazed at the pictures of the beautiful butterflies.

That November, we celebrated our first American holiday, Thanksgiving. On that day, everyone ate turkey, bread stuffing, sweet potatoes and pumpkin pie. As we were still very Italian, there was no holiday without pasta so the two meals were combined.

Nonna had decided that our feast would include a fresh turkey. Elisa and I accompanied her downtown to a fresh poultry store which was about a mile or so away. There, we witnessed quite an animation of Nonna flapping her arms to mimic a bird. After much ado, the vendor understood that she wanted a live turkey to take home. From what we could comprehend from that very comical interaction, they were not permitted to let live poultry leave their store. She even explained, in Italian, about the many chickens she had butchered in her lifetime. As an alternative, she demanded to be present to ensure that it was done properly, but that too was impossible. Although Nonna remained a bit peeved, she had a good sense of humor. The three of us laughed all the way home as we carried our groceries and a very dead fresh turkey.

In between the heavy snow storms that were common for that area in November, when the sidewalks were clear, I tagged along on walks with Mom, Zia Elena and Elisa to acquaint ourselves with the neighborhood. A "for sale" sign in front of a house we passed caught Mom's eye.

Over dinner the very next day, Mom and Pop revealed that they had found the perfect house for us. Many friends had suggested homes to us that were within the Italian communities. Pop wanted us to be out of the upstairs apartment and into our own home. At the same time, he wanted to remain within walking distance to our nonni, work and school. Above all, he wished for us to learn to speak English which would be facilitated by living in an American community. That line of thinking suited me just fine since I spoke neither English nor Italian!

One month after arriving in America we moved into the first home that we had ever owned. We were all beyond proud. Being newcomers in the country, even with our decent down payment, we were unlikely to qualify for a bank loan. Fortunately for us, another family in our community who had emigrated from Italy years earlier, ran an established business to help other Italian families like ours, by providing mortgage loans.

Our new home, all brick, was on the left side of the double with a lovely front porch. The structure and model of the residences in the neighborhood were almost all identical. Each of them were separated by an access strip that included a concrete walkway on each side that led to the respective back yard. That space between each footpath was decorated with shrubs, flowers and grass. The proximity between each dwelling made it possible to converse with neighbors from their own porches.

Two windows brightened each room in the house. The kitchen had an entire wall of pure white cabinets to store all of the china that we had not yet bought and it came with our very first refrigerator! We were told it was a very old model but we did not care.

A tiny room connected to the kitchen that we called the "shandy" kept our winter coats and jackets handy while it also provided access to the backyard. My brothers and I immediately though of Mr. Gernez, when we discovered our own "telephone room." We hadn't; it was our dining room with a lone black rotary phone sitting smack in the middle of it.

To the side was an open staircase leading up to three bedrooms and a bathroom. Nonno had told us that we should expect hot water in all of the homes. All the same, the water in the bathtub was tested to make sure. The bedroom that Elisa and I shared overlooked the back yard. A staircase hidden inside our closet led to an attic. Pop joked that since the attic was not heated, those two rooms would be used for storage. We giggled at that, because we knew that we didn't even have enough furniture to fill the rest of the rooms.

A staircase accessible from the kitchen descended into a spacious basement. A large utility room with another exit to the back yard housed the washing machine and a huge porcelain utility sink. A huge oil tank took over the smaller area at the far end of basement. We were told the tank was filled with oil and the furnace beside it pushed heat through the radiators in each room of the house to keep us warm all day and all night. Pop said it was more house than we needed but it came at a great price and in a perfect location.

Pop's little haven was outside under the blue sky. He joked about converting both patches of grass in the back yard into a vegetable garden. Mom had already limited him to the smaller area adjacent to the garage that was accessible from the alleyway. We shared the detached double garage with our neighbor. A narrow flower bed with the most beautiful roses abutted the fence separating our yard from that of our neighbors on either side.

Our home was furnished with our beds, kitchen table and six chairs that Mom and Pop had bought during our first weeks in America. Several months later, Pop exchanged more cash to buy living room furniture. Zio Antimo drove us all downtown to the Goodman Furniture Store. Pop turned it into a family adventure when he invited us to help pick out colors. In all of the excitement, he also surprised us by purchasing a black and white Emerson TV.

The mood changed sharply when Pop pulled a huge wad of cash from a zippered pouch to close the sale. Paled, the clerk politely indicated that a different form of payment was desirable. Pop was mortified that his hard earned money was not good in that establishment. Zio handled the translation, but similar to Nonna's interaction at the live poultry store, it resulted in a complete misunderstanding on both sides.

In essence, the vendor did not want to keep the cash in the building or at home overnight. Pop claimed he was not a thief and had no intention of returning to steal the money, although, I am pretty sure that there was no attempt to translate that part. Pop did not perceive any of this as his problem, he simply wanted to pay and leave. That dialogue, back and forth, lasted long after the store closed. The vendor finally gave up. Merry Christmas to us!

The rest of the rooms stayed empty along with our dining room that was able to remain our "telephone room" for a while longer, but we had the things we needed and the TV found its place.

Our first Christmas in America was fabulous. Reminding us that we lived in the Christmas city of Bethlehem, a perfect view of the ninety-one foot star on the hillside of South Mountain could be seen from the end of our street. It stayed lit all through the holidays.

It was the first year that we decorated a tree that found its perfect spot next to the fireplace in the living room. The fireplace was completely decked out with Christmas cards from new and old friends in America, France and Italy. The collage included cards from Nadine and Danila. We had promised one another to write but the mail was dishearteningly slow and I missed them more with each passing day.

In America, the *Befana* came on Christmas day and luckily for me, it was a coal free holiday. After breakfast, we walked to our nonni's house just down the street where we all celebrated together. For all major holidays and special days, Nonno gifted each grandchild a crisp $10 bill that went directly into a piggy bank.

The changes in our lives brought an abundance of happiness along with an equivalent amount of apprehension. Elisa spent most nights at the home of my aunt and uncle. Elisa and Zia Elena had become very close. We saw one another over dinner since Mom still cooked for all the workers at our house. Each evening I asked her to stay home. Her response was always "maybe" or "we'll see" but she never did. Cognizant that she profoundly missed her friends from *Fenain* and our zii seemed attentive to her, I didn't press it. Nevertheless, I felt alone and deeply missed her.

The language barrier was significant. Joining Pop in France felt so much easier for us. He had already been living there for a year and had ensured everything was ready for us. In America, we not only needed to learn to speak English, Italian had also become a priority in order to communicate with our nonni. While we looked to the adults for help, they turned to us. For Mom, Pop and Elisa, learning a new language for the second time was even more problematic.

The middle school nearby offered English lessons for foreigners. Pop, Zio and Elisa attended together. Being the youngest in the class, Elisa picked things up very quickly. The instructor recommended a more advanced class for her that was offered at another school farther away. As we were in a strange land, plus we had no easy means of transportation, Pop would not allow it. One would not think it possible, but our parents had become even stricter in America. They did not know the area like *Fenain* or *City Heurteau*, they did not know a lot of people and Elisa was a girl!

As for me, I stayed secretly relieved that chairs were not assigned by merit because school assignments were still non-existent. At the same time, a sadness settled in my heart knowing that I would never see the proud look on Pop's face at the school awards again.

Nonno Alfredo, who also struggled with the communication, understood my distress and suggested that we help one another. Our lessons were set for ten o'clock on Saturday mornings at his house. It was a perfect plan, I was thrilled to learn and he was delighted to have an interested student. Using Alberto Pecorini's *Grammar-Encyclopedia: English-Italian for Italians in the United States*, Nonno explained the difference between *Orsaresi* and Italian. Accordingly, it became an "Ameritalian" lesson. He was an extraordinary and very caring grandfather. The most enjoyable part of our get-togethers were the stories that he enriched our time with.

Four months after arriving in the United States, a spot finally opened up at the school with a foreign student program. The school was far which obligated me to take a school bus. As eager as I was to learn, riding the bus frightened me, starting yet another school worried me and, once again, I would not know anyone.

To lessen my anxieties, Nonno accompanied me to the bus stop on my first day, just in case the driver asked questions. Most of my apprehensions dissolved quickly. The bus driver simply greeted me with a smile. The teacher in the program was very nice.

Our group included seven students from different parts of the world: Greece, Portugal, Puerto Rico and one from *Orsara*. My assigned fourth grade classroom was simply for roll call, then I was immediately released to spend the rest of the day in the program.

While there, I had an opportunity to meet an author, Ruth Nulton Moore, who visited our school after publishing, *Frisky, the playful pony*. Although I understood practically nothing, she talked to me at length and autographed a copy with: "Someday soon, I know you will be able to read this book. I hope you will enjoy it as much as I enjoy horses."

Changes were in the air for Mom too. During our first spring in America, she decided to contribute to the family financials, although, I believed that she was covertly tired of preparing large meals every day for the entire family. Pop was not a fan of Mom working since Gino was not of school age. Additionally, our first winter in America had been very hard on him. He never complained, but the deep hacking coughs coming from his tiny little body were horrifying. He suffered from bronchial problems that doctors said needed time to heal.

Nonno was very supportive of Mom's determination to work, so he had accompanied her to Lehigh Dress, a factory at walking distance. Nonno worked there part time to weed, clip roses and trim small bushes around the perimeter of the building. Their only vacancy was for a zipper setter. Since it was very specialized work, it was often difficult to fill. Other than my grandfather's recommendation, Mom had no formal training or prior experience in America. Instead, she offered to demonstrate her skills, for which, she was hired on the spot.

My progressing English vocabulary designated me as the family interpreter. Accordingly, after school, I accompanied Mom across the alley to the home of Mr. and Mrs. Murcic, a kind retired couple who loved Gino. The couple immediately understood Mom's desire to work. Before making the request, they offered to care for Gino until the start of kindergarten.

Once everything was in order, she shared her news with Pop. Worried about his reaction, I stayed close. As predicted, he blurted out, "No!" Mom retorted that we needed the money, she was capable and wanted to contribute. Plus, Gino would be well taken care of. Pop reluctantly conceded as he had no further argument.

Mom no longer cooked for all the workers. Each family migrated to their respective homes after work. Our evenings became calmer and our family dinners quickly took the familiar similarity of those we remembered from France. The six of us had time to talk with one another, and our parents were interested in hearing about our day.

My added bonus was that my sister spent nights at home. We quickly fell into our normal seats around the kitchen table which, oddly enough, was not wide enough for me and Gino. Despite having the shortest legs in the family, by the end of dinner we were both crouched at the very edge of our chairs in a silent kicking war under the table.

Pop took his place at the far end of the kitchen near the window where he had a perfect view of the blue sky and the full landscape to see all the comings and goings in the house. On Saturday nights, he taught us the Italian card games of briscola and scopa.

Sundays and holiday dinners were always reserved for our extended family. We alternated weekly between the houses of Zii, my nonni and ours. Elisa's eighteenth birthday also set a new precedent to celebrate special days.

My parents reintroduced the record player that shared its place with the telephone in our still empty dining room. Once we were able to furnish it, the dance floor materialized by simply pushing the furniture to the side.

Some Sunday afternoons, we gathered around the table to play Black Jack or Italian bingo called *tombola*. We played for nickels and dimes. The jackpot included a few quarters. For the children, a benefit of sharing tombola cards with Nonno Alfredo meant he paid for the cards then gave up all of the winnings to his "partner."

When old stories surfaced that made conversations more serious, the children were sent elsewhere to play. We soundlessly left and waited it out. No one played and no one ever called us back. When we heard calmness, we returned to a fresh pot of coffee and calmer conversations.

Our first summer in America marked the end of my first school year. Already knowing the answer, I asked, "Who will take care of us during the summer since everyone works?" Surprised the question even needed to be asked, Mom simply replied, "You're in charge of the house and your brothers." Having just turned ten, I understood. My sister had taken care of me, it was my turn to take care of my brothers. My real worry was that being closer to their age, they did not listen to me like we listened to Elisa.

On my last day of school, my teacher said that my English had progressed well enough to re-enter my community school in the fall. My joy transformed to beyond crushed, later that day, when my report card revealed a "promotion" to fourth grade. Reality had finally set in. My work there was specifically to learn the English language. Fourth grade was still waiting for me. Nevertheless, that devastation needed to be on hold. My more immediate dilemma was to figure out what it meant to be in charge of the kids and the house.

Over the summer, my English communication steadily improved. Among the siblings, we spoke mostly in English. With our parents, it was a cocktail of English, Italian, French and a few made up words. For purely selfish reasons, I created lesson plans for a summer school program at home. Gino and Alfredo, who were both already fluent in English and remembered very little French, were my very reluctant students. School work was slated for the mornings with playtime in the afternoons.

Needless to say, the boys were irritated not only with my plan of study, but also for being stuck in the house. They stayed engaged for a bit until they wanted to play, then they staged a mutiny. Hoping for a democratic resolution to our problem and having watched plenty of episodes of *The Case of Perry Mason*,[20] I concocted a contract defining our responsibilities which they agreed to sign. That too was short-lived. Ongoing mutinies forced me to prepare contracts to not breach contracts. Eventually, they won.

Playtime was outside. There were quite a few children on our street close to Alfredo and Gino's age. Alfredo loved to play outside and had made a lot of friends. Gino was little and very sociable, our friends became his friends too. Our street was less busy than others around us since it was one-way, however, it was crowded with cars parked on both sides. Children typically played in the less travelled alley in the back of our house. There, the boys played baseball,

---

[20] *The Case of Perry Mason*: Television series of 30 episodes of 90 minutes each. Perry Mason was a highly successful lawyer in Los Angeles

basketball or just hung out. I played hopscotch, hula-hoop or jump rope with some of the girls in the neighborhood.

We had a swing set in our yard but most of the time, we sat on our front porch with friends talking and laughing. It was not long before our front porch became a main congregation spot on our block. On the Saturdays when Mom baked bread, the first loaf out of the oven was sliced and shared among whomever was on the porch. On nice evenings and weekends, Pop, who had no shortage of stories to share with our attentive neighbors, also took refuge on the front porch.

It was during one of those porch chatters that I discovered a dentist office had recently opened in our neighborhood. Intrigued with the notion of teeth cleanings, especially if it prevented more silver from entering my mouth without giving up the sweets, I asked Pop about taking me and my brothers. He asked if anyone was complaining about pain, made a few jokes like he always did, but he did not say no. Instead, he asked me to collect more information, including cost. The next day, with my brothers in tow, we walked to the dentist office for the necessary details and scheduled the appointment.

Returning on our designated day, we were refused service since we were not accompanied by an adult. My brothers took my hand to leave. Obstinate, I refused. In protest, we sat and waited for a very long time until the dentist finally surfaced to resolve the situation. As for my justification, I explained that my parents could not take time off from work, they did not speak English so they will need to talk with me anyway, I was responsible, we had permission and I had the exact amount of money for all three of us. We agreed in principle. He cleaned our teeth but specified that we must be accompanied by an adult on future visits.

Our neighborhood was full of almost everything we needed. A half block down the street, mid-way between our house and our nonni, was a hardware store, a barber shop, a doctor's office and the local drugstore that also sold soda, ice cream and candy. Everything we needed. Mom left me money for when the boys needed haircuts or we needed milk, bread or popsicles. The kind patrons at the stores knew everyone by name.

On a typical summer day, we ate cereal for breakfast and sandwiches for lunch. When we found an old recipe book tucked in the back of the pantry left by the previous owner, we attempted some. Sometimes when we substituted ingredients, it worked other times not. One afternoon, noticing a chicken thawing, motivated me to help with dinner too. Having watched Mom make chicken and roasted potatoes a bazillion times, how hard could it be? For the six of us, I considered the ten pound bag of potatoes in the pantry and peeled its full content. After seasoning the chicken with salt, pepper, parsley, garlic, olive oil and Romano cheese, I sliced the potatoes which formed a massive mound. It was clear that they would not fit in the roasting pan. My mother was going to kill me!

Dinner that evening came with compliments, although, it was noted that there were way too many potatoes. Thankfully, they were not aware of the other half buried in the backyard!

Occasionally, on Saturdays I was permitted to walk to the community swimming pool near the park, provided I was in the company of a friend that my parents knew well. Observing children all lined up at the diving board, I took my place. That day, I quickly discovered that diving required significantly more skill than I possessed, like actually knowing how to swim. After sinking straight to the bottom and hitting my head, the lifeguard pulled me out of the pool. A bit of choking and a small bump on my forehead did not require a report to my parents or a trip to the hospital. There was no concern on my part about my friend snitching about this incident to my parents. They would not understand her and it was not something that I had planned to translate properly.

The following weekend, Mom surprised me with a new swimsuit. Eager to wear it, I mistakenly told Mom that I was going swimming. Naturally, Mom said "no" although I remained convinced that "asking" would have had the same result! In my mind, it was absurd to get a new swimsuit if one was not allowed to go the pool, so the insisting persisted.

As it turned out, my friend had told her parents about the pool incident. By word of mouth: her parents told a friend, who told a friend who worked with Zia, told Zia, who told my mother…Voila! An important revelation for me was that, one way or another, the truth always came out.

Mom was angry and launched into: "You could have been seriously injured, or worse, died!" The conversation ended with a few reflexive whacks on my head with the aluminum roasting pan that she happened to be holding in her hand. That day, I learned what a real *paliatone* was. The worst part was having to return the pan to my nonna. Its dents exposed as I handed it to her, said everything. She hugged me while I cried a little more over figs and a café au lait.

As the summer came to an end, I was anxious to get fourth grade started and finished. Alfredo and I, hand-in-hand, walked down our street to Stevens school. Children were clearly important in America because they had their own crossing guard to keep them safe. Mr. Huff lived a few doors from ours. We respectfully waited for his signal to cross while my thoughts told him that having walked for longer distances and having crossed railroad tracks on my own, help wasn't needed and I was perfectly capable of keeping my little brother safe.

Co-ed recess now felt more normal. From the courtyard, we waved to Nonno who was almost always perched on his patio across the street. Mid-day, hand-in-hand with my brother, we crossed the road for lunch. Whether it was leftovers, provolone cheese, prosciutto or mortadella with homemade bread, Nonno always had it ready on the table. When the peaches in his garden ripened, he sliced them in a cup and poured a little of wine on them. We ate the peaches and he drank the wine.

Homework was another story. My English continued to improve whereas my written work remained a struggle. Intensely disheartened, I always procrastinated doing my homework by watching TV or dilly-dallying on the front porch with my friends, but it always got done. That stalling annoyed my sister who subtly nudged close enough for me to hear her sing:

"My beloved little sister. Oh, oh, oh…
Come a bit closer and listen to me. Oh, oh, oh…
I love you dearly but you disappoint me because you do nothing at school.
Oh, oh, oh." [21]

That song drove me absolutely insane. While my friends were unfamiliar with the words, she knew that translating them would be humiliating. In essence, she shamed me into spending more time on my studies.

My favorite subject was math for obvious reasons. Math was math in any language. The rest of the work remained challenging. My first math test yielded an excellent mark. The teacher's request to return it with parental signature thrilled me.

The reaction from my parents however, was completely unexpected. They questioned the need for a signature if there was nothing wrong with it. There was some ranting around the red letter "C" on each problem. Red in their world was bad and my explanation of "C" designating them as correct went on deaf ears. The next morning, the paper still sat on the kitchen table unsigned. Exasperated, I practiced Mom's signature on the back of a napkin a few times while Alfredo readied for school. It did not appear particularly hard, I had seen it a million times on official documents.

Confessing my deed that evening, she smiled when I showed her an almost perfect forgery. In America, the school required notes for essentially everything. The next time Alfredo was sick, Mom asked me to prepare and sign his note. In fact, all future school papers and notes, good or bad, for me and my brothers were signed by me.

---

[21] French song, "A toi de choisir" by Richard Anthony meaning it is your choice to make.

Another school novelty was an annual parent-teacher conference in late fall. Pop demanded to know what I had done to warrant his presence. After persisting with every parent met with teachers regarding their child's progress without the student present, he reluctantly agreed. However, he expected me to be by his side as the interpreter. That was not negotiable and I really wanted him to go.

Naturally, my teacher did not expect to see me at that session. When I translated her preference to have a one-on-one, Pop asked if I had done something wrong. My very vivid recollection of the experience at the furniture store encouraged me to translate that he was happy to meet her and that she may freely discuss my studies.

Still uncomfortable, she expressed that I was doing fine and wished to reschedule for another time without me. In turn, I translated that I was doing well but my English still needed improvement. In my heart, there was no question that this was a complete waste of everyone's time. Without much left to say, we wrapped up quickly. Pop respectfully tipped his hat, then he gave a half bow to end the first and last conference that my parents were ever informed about.

Even in America, autumn meant winemaking. While it too was very festive, it was a whole lot easier. Each year, a truck loaded with grapes from California circled to those Italians in the area who made their own wine. Nonno was equipped with several oak barrels, a wine press and a boat load of glass gallons, so he, Pop and Zio made wine together in his basement. Nonno tested it often with the same revelation, "It's almost ready!" Real ready, included a wine tasting celebration for the adults and ice cream sandwiches all around.

Over time, Pop wanted to be more mobile. Some of the things we needed access to were not within a reasonable walking distance. Mobylettes or bicycles were unsafe in our busy streets. Zio graciously drove us for our weekly grocery shopping. Nevertheless, Pop never liked to impose on others, he wanted to be more independent.

In conversation, little Gino mentioned to the Murcic's that Pop was learning to drive. With that, Mr. Murcic offered Pop his 1949 Oldsmobile, a car he had not driven for many years. It had a hand brake to accommodate Mr. Murcic's polio handicap which needed to be switched. Other than that, it was an excellent starter car. He refused money for it and would not take "no" for an answer. Pop, who never took anything for nothing, repaid them by doing yard work.

Almost every night after dinner, a friend from work assisted Pop with the driver manual and the road training. Afterwards, Pop turned the manual over to me to continue quizzing him. A few weeks later, he had his driver's license.

By spring of 1968, our extended family grew when Pop's sister, Zia Concetta from *Orsara* joined us in America. We were thrilled to see our cousins Alfredo, whom we called Freddy, Mike and Netta.

Zia and Pop were deliriously comical together. On the evening of their arrival, Zia abruptly stood up from the dinner table, fanning herself as she complained about the heat. She began to unzip her dress in the middle of the kitchen. Pop was horrified which made her laugh even harder. She revealed another dress underneath, and another, and another. They did not fit in her suitcase. Refusing to leave them behind, she simply wore all five of them!

Zia Concetta immediately started her job. There was no shortage of factories. The entire block next to ours was lined on both sides with huge red brick factories for dresses, pajamas and thread. She worked with Zia Elena at the dress factory. Netta worked with Elisa who had recently changed jobs to work at the pajama factory. Elisa had made some nice friends since our arrival in America and was thrilled not only to have another friend but a cousin close to her age.

The rules regarding spending time at the home of our friends remained unchanged. They were always welcome at our house as long as they were not boys, so Elisa and I invited friends over often. What we found annoying was that Pop told endless stories about life in his native village, France or whatever else. Good or bad, they always sounded like fairytales that were inhabited by fictitious characters living in a different era. Naturally, his stories effortlessly took center stage while cutting into our socializing time. Worse, many of our friends loved listening to him, broken English and all.

A serious disruption in our life was something that none of us had anticipated in America, the land of opportunity. A strike at the company where Pop worked took him to the picket line in solidarity with his colleagues every day. In between his protesting obligations, he took odd jobs here and there. Mom started sewing our clothes again. The crate with her sewing machine, which had been lost in transit from France, was eventually recovered after two years. While some items such as Mom's favorite American dress went missing, the rose silk bedspread thankfully made its way into her arms.

We were never short of food. An Italian friend of Pop had started a vegetable garden years prior on communal property that the Italians called *tomba*. He offered Pop a parcel of land large enough to plant tomatoes, peppers, beans and Swiss chard.

The word *tomba* always bothered me because there was no suitable translation for it. It was not until many years later that I learned the area had been a city dump. *Tomba* was the closest *Orsaresi* pronunciation to the word dump. Although none of them owned that land, there was clearly a leader, opportunities were by invitation only, and everyone always followed the rules. They even built a little hut on the property to house their tools.

Pop was out of work long enough that he was deeply alarmed about making our house payment. He always managed to put a small amount of money in savings, just in case. But after a while, even with all earnings in our house already going into the common pot, it was not enough. Obviously, we were all distressed about the potential of losing our home. One afternoon, while commiserating with my siblings, we remembered our piggy banks. Combined, it was sufficient to make up the difference needed to pay our mortgage.

The strike ended a few months later. Nevertheless, Pop kept his second job during the warmer months doing construction, just in case. Plus, the extra cash was always good. He worked for a friend of a friend directly after his regular job. We still all ate dinner together, just a little later.

Our adventure to America offered us a new world full of many wonderful opportunities. Our lives were more comfortable than we could ever have imagined. Pop told us that with more opportunities came more responsibilities, sacrifices and obligations. Everyone who was able to work had a job. My parents and my sister worked hard to make sure that we had what we needed. I wanted to do my part, however small, to preserve our family cohesion which was our strength.

My progress in school significantly improved. The first chapter book that I fully read in America was *The Count of Monto Cristo* by Alexandre Dumas. Determined, it was read and re-read several times before fully understanding the entire storyline. Once again, I loved to read and read many books.

In mid-November 1969, Pete Conrad and Alan Bean of Apollo 12 walked "Oceans of Storms" on the moon. Students were all crowded in the hallway of our school watching this world event unfold live on television. It was beyond thrilling to understand what was happening while it was actually happening.

Finishing sixth grade with excellent marks didn't lessen the disappointment in myself. My overall school performance weighed heavily on me. Progress had been slower than ever imagined. To express my thoughts out loud felt ungrateful. There were so many things to be happy about, but at the same time, a part of me felt isolated and lost.

In the fall, I would begin middle school. It was a little over a mile walk from our home. In that new school, I will no longer be the little girl who did not speak English. It was my opportunity for a fresh start.

6

An adolescent in America

In late summer 1969, I met my "big brother" Dominic. He and Elisa had stumbled upon one another at a small diner frequented by the factory workers in the area. Over the course of that week, Dominic clocked out from the silk mill then drove his convertible, an old 1960 red Chevy Impala, up and down our street. If he spotted Elisa on the porch, he stopped. The porch was not a habitual hangout for her but this week was oddly different. He sat inside his parked car while Elisa stood on the sidewalk by the car window where they talked for hours.

At night, I refused to switch off our bedroom light that was conveniently located directly above my head, until Elisa shared the gist of their chitchats. The eight years of disparity in our age never separated us. As adolescent girls, we routinely commiserated about our parents' excessive rigor and protective shield that felt like a hindrance to our independence.

We knew that behavior was, in part, tied to our parents' childhood in a culture from another part of the world. In France, there had been more consideration since they knew the families of our small communities. Our respective fathers all worked at the mine and Pop knew almost everyone. America held too many unknowns. We didn't know the families, the city was large, the society was more liberal and boys sometimes appeared a bit bizarre and disrespectful to them.

Our conversations always ended with a shared exasperation concerning our pleas that even in *Orsara* and in the Nord, they had progressed. They simply did not care. Casual dating, for instance, was a foreign concept to Pop. Frankly, it was not even a part of his universe. To avoid the craziness and to spare Dominic from the wraths of Pop, Elisa had simply told Dominic that she was not interested in dating him. Being more direct and prone to push boundaries just a little closer to the edge, I quickly offered some advice, "Dominic is nice and he doesn't appear to be going away, so just tell Pop you want to date him."

She discounted my advice while Dominic ignored her rejections. By Friday, Dominic changed his approach. He parked his car then joined us on the porch. Sensing Elisa's tension, I kept vigil for Pop who oddly had not been on the porch that entire week. He never missed much, so there was no doubt he was nearby and knew exactly what was going on.

The topic of conversation during Sunday dinner by everyone, except Elisa, was obviously Dominic. He was Italian and Pop already knew his two older brothers. At a very young age, Dominic had already dealt with substantive life hardships. His mother, a widow, and her three boys had emigrated from Sicily when Dominic was nine years old. At the age of thirteen, he lost his mother in a horrific car accident. They were returning from a shopping trip downtown by bus to buy Dominic a suit for his oldest brother's wedding. Hand-in-hand, they had stepped off at their designated stop and walked around the front of the bus to cross the street. Meanwhile, a car drove around the stationary vehicle and struck her. After the accident, Dominic lived with his brother for a few years. As soon as he turned sixteen, he found employment while he attended high school. It paid for meals, incidentals and the bedroom that he rented a few blocks from his job. Pop was not trusting of any boy who approached his daughters, yet his tone revealed respect toward Dominic.

We were finishing dinner when the doorbell rang. As usual, my brothers and I raced for the door. Equally thrilled and panicked to be face-to-face with Dominic, we rudely left him at the door. Worried about Pop's reaction, Gino sheepishly whispered to Elisa, "It's him." Pop, who never missed anything, matter-of-factly responded in Italian, "Where are your manners? Invite him in."

Elisa and I eyed each other. There was no choice except to invite that poor guy into a war zone. The only person in the room with any semblance of tranquility was Pop. After some uncomfortable introductions, Dominic joined us around the kitchen table where everything happened in our family. My brothers eventually went outside to play while I stayed glued to my chair as if any part of their conversation was any of my business.

Dominic wasn't very talkative which turned out great since Pop was. Trivial chatter amid a mix of Dominic's Sicilian dialect, a lot of *Orsaresi* and a little bit of English went on for hours. The darkness peering through the kitchen window called this day almost over and forced the evaded subject. Then, it toppled like an avalanche. Pop stood firm on his position of casual dating and launched into a mixed language tirade ending with, "It does not exist in our house and that is not negotiable." My sister was mortified as Pop carried on. For his closing argument, he made very clear that if Dominic was serious, he could date his daughter, otherwise, it was best to simply leave and never return.

Although Dominic was a bit terrified, he evenly voiced that he understood what Pop was saying while delicately articulating that there were no guarantees in life. What he did promise Pop was to be respectful of both him and his daughter. Even though Pop was sufficiently satisfied, he still emphasized his rules, which even in his broken English could not be misunderstood: "No can go out every night" because of our family obligations. When they did go out, she must "be ome eleven o'clock, no eleven and one minoot." Thankfully, Pop did not condone chaperoning. With nothing else left to say, Elisa accompanied Dominic to the front door where they talked in private for no more than a minute.

We silently finished washing the dinner dishes that were still stacked near the sink and called it a night. My heart ached for my sister. All my nightly questions found their answers before they were asked. She admitted telling him that she understood if he chose not to return, although her eyes were saying otherwise before they closed and wished that day gone. In that moment, I had resolved never to marry because I would never bring a boy home.

The day after the interrogation and forever later, a seventh chair was set around our family table. Dominic cherished my sister, then and always. In turn, we all adored Dominic long before he and Elisa decided to marry the following summer. They included me and my brothers on most of their outings. They took us to the park, the zoo and swimming at the lake. We were delighted to go, at the same time, it provided them more occasions to be together.

Dominic surprised Alfredo and Gino with their first baseball glove. When Gino slipped on his glove, it was a very emotional moment. His eyes met Dominic's to ask why? Dominic, glassy eyed, simply said, "All little boys should have their own baseball glove." He helped to make us all a little more American.

With one another's support, we were, for the most part, well-rooted in our community. On the other hand, the social aspects of life had become more complicated for me and my brothers as we grew older and sought more independence. Uprooting twice forced all of us to grow up faster in many ways. We always helped one another and accepted our responsibilities and obligations unequivocally. With Pop, we also all learned to only interpret half of what he said, especially if he was angry. He used colorful language that we were not allowed to use, so he must have known that we filtered other things too.

Accompanying my parents, just in case they needed an interpreter, to fill out their documents and forms, I learned more about insurance, unemployment benefits, paying bills and banking than many adults. Pop never liked to be dependent on anyone so he found creative ways to do things for himself. He once asked me to write down all of the possible numerical denominations on a piece of paper that he conveniently tucked in his wallet as a reference for when he wrote checks.

The real source of our frustration with Pop lay with his unwillingness to even attempt to embrace the changing times. It no longer coincided with his family values. We were not French, Italian or American. We were the Russo family with Russo rules in a mélange of "francoameritalian" culture! In the words of my baby brother, "Pop was Pop. He should have come with a manual." Even with all the hoopla, what was never in question was that in life, family always came first.

Years after the company strike, Pop still worked multiple jobs. He had kept his part-time construction work during the warmer seasons, just in case. His network of loyal and devoted *paisanos* always volunteered to help one another with home improvement projects or whenever some extra muscle was needed. Money was rarely exchanged. Typically, the cost was a sandwich, a beer and the unspoken promise to be there for one another.

For the same reason that Pop kept his part-time job, he tended to the large vegetable garden at *tomba*. In the smaller patch near the garage, he planted a few vegetable plants, herbs to have handy day-to-day and a fig tree. Our fig shoot had come from Nonno Alfredo's tree which had originated from *Orsara* many years prior.

Our cuisine fused Sicilian zucchini and giant green beans that Dominic introduced to us. Alfredo was simply fascinated by the enormous size of those vegetables that grew up to three feet long. He and a friend that he had recruited took this peculiarity to our local newspaper, the <u>Bethlehem Globe Times</u>, who published an article on that phenomenon of nature along with a photo of the boys.

In the larger vegetable garden, Pop planted over one hundred tomato plants. During the fall and winter, our window sills in the "shandy" were covered with seeds on paper towels drying in the sun. In the spring, the tiny seedlings were squeezed in that same space until Pop transplanted them. On Saturday mornings, Pop asked my brothers to assist with watering, as if that was ever a real option. They filled buckets with water from a spigot at a residence down the street that Pop had made an agreement with. With the aid of a small red wagon, they pulled it up and down the hill to water all the plants. At harvest, all three of us were invited to fill bushels and bushels of tomatoes. Occasionally, to break the monotony, we stole moments for rotten tomato battles when Pop was looking elsewhere. My aim had never been good so a bad strike to Pop's head ended our games. He took it in stride, but we were not stupid enough to risk it again. At least not on the same day.

Lucky for me, an allergic reaction to tomato plants spared me from harvest but not from canning. There was shared silent seething when we found tomatoes spread over newspaper covering the basement floor. It was a firm indicator that quality family canning time was going to fill our weekend while other kids our age would likely be outside playing or going to the movies.

To facilitate canning, we had installed a second stove and sink in our basement. It also came in handy during the hot summer days since we did not have air conditioning. That allowed us to prepare and eat our meals in a cooler part of the house. We installed a second bathroom to avoid going up two flights of stairs which also simplified our tight morning shower schedules. On weekends, Pop's shaving ritual in our basement bathroom reminded me of our days in France. Those days of long ago sitting on the table in our laundry room while he shaved using a tiny mirror over the washing machine. It took forever because he was meticulous and he kept stopping to talk. Even now, always afraid to miss something, he shaved with the bathroom door slightly ajar to join in our chats.

English had improved substantially for my parents, but habits kept our conversations a mélange of English, Italian, a little French and a few made up words. We knew what words they knew and didn't, the language simply flowed accordingly. It was a tad confusing when American friends were present but they understood the gist of the conversation.

Over many dinners, my brothers and I tried to teach my parents the "H" sound. With Pop, it was hit or miss depending on whether he stopped long enough to think before he spoke. Mom, on the other hand, could make the sound only if it was not attached to a word. She sounded it out, over and over, "Huh…huh…huh…orse" (horse). It was futile, on the other hand, we had a ton of laughs together and had to agree that there was no "H" sound in Mom's vocabulary.

Much like our dinners, free time was family time. We celebrated Italian, French and American holidays. Our parents faithfully kept up with family and friends overseas. Additionally, in September 1969, we purchased our first new car, a stunning maroon LTD Ford with a black vinyl top. The black interior seats were protected by plastic to better preserve them.

With this more reliable car, Mom and Pop rekindled friendships and reciprocated far away visits in New Jersey, Massachusetts and Vermont. In honor of Pop's friend from *Escaudain*, they travelled to New Hemisphere to visit Mr. Luongo's sister.

Much had changed in our lives while so many other things remained the same. In our home, the rules for boys and girls were very clear. There was nothing equal about them. None of us liked or agreed with the parental rigor that seemed unreasonable and inexplicable. Nevertheless, we were all in solidarity and wallowed in silence, otherwise, no one would be allowed to do anything.

In some ways it was harder for Alfredo and Gino because they had no frame for where this cultural difference came from. They had never lived in Italy and had little recollection of our life in France. They were growing up with American friends and had more American influence. For them, entering our home sometimes felt like entering a foreign country. They had a lot of friends and joined various organized team sports in our community. Gino played little league minors, a baseball team sponsored by the Democratic Club. Both he and Alfredo played soccer for the Portuguese Club.

Organized activities were not something my parents were accustomed to so they never grasped the concept of participating in them. Occasionally we asked them but they were always too busy working at their jobs, the garden or doing something else that they felt needed to be done. They never offered and we finally stopped asking. Sometimes, we heard them joke about working in their parents' fields at the age of twelve. It seemed natural that they had stopped treating us like children very young. For us, we were stuck between multiple worlds where we were neither children nor adults. Thankfully, the boys either walked to their function or they had great friends that they were able to tag along with.

For me, there was the added complication of being born girl. In Pop's mind, daughters left home when they married and they dated when they were ready to get married. Interestingly, with Elisa's marriage, Pop made an immediate shift. He never meddled and was respectful of their decisions as a couple. This caused an abundance of confusion for me. From my perspective, if Pop was able to instantly make that transition, there was no doubt that he understood. I simply wanted him to trust us a little more with a bit more independence.

Pop always stayed informed. On weekends, he read the newspaper from cover to cover. We believed that he only understood half of what he read, but he discovered the school honor roll. In middle and high school, scholastic merit was recognized in our local newspaper at the end of each quarter. He found my class listing and stumbled upon my name. When he read it aloud, I saw that flash of pride shining in his eyes, it was the same look I recalled from the school awards ceremony in *Fenain* forever ago.

My three years of middle school in America were absolutely magnificent and were, without a doubt, my happiest school years in America. I had made some amazing friends. My classes were still hard but I stayed determined and was doing well. At the same time, I was perplexed to pass the chorus tryout with my clear inability to carry a tune. Our weekly rehearsals were immediately after school, allowing me to return home early enough to help Mom with whatever she needed. I loved being a part of this club so I lip sang at our concerts to avoid losing my spot.

The school was multi-cultural and included a substantive student population of migrants. Middle school was also when foreign languages were introduced to our curriculum. Our choices were French, German or Spanish. During the first year, students were exposed to one language per quarter. By the fourth iquarter, the student commenced with their chosen language to pursue.

Naturally, I was thrilled to register for French even though it came with some teasing from classmates for taking an easy class. What had been really disheartening for me was that except for a few words mixed in our conversations, we had entirely abandoned speaking it at home. A huge takeaway from those French classes was the connection that allowed the rules of English grammar to finally click for me.

Our only non-co-ed classes were gymnastics, workshop for the boys and home economics for the girls. Each quarter, the girls alternated between cooking, sewing and social etiquette. Classes that, from my perspective, were a complete waste of my time: I was always too clumsy to be the slightest bit athletic, I had cooked since the age of ten. As for sewing, I had already mastered Mom's sewing machine. Etiquette covered some fundamentals for young girls since we were all approaching sixteen. That class offered students approaches to respectfully interact with parents in regards to dating. Should your date wait in his car, toot the horn, or come to the door to greet your parents when picking you up? None of which was relevant for me since dating was not permitted.

A genuine complication for me was that the course included a multipage homework assignment to engage our parents in a dialogue about expectations. Not only was the assignment impossible for me to complete, there was no easy way to broach that subject with either my parents or my teacher.

When I found the courage to privately express to my teacher that it was not a subject that my parents would discuss with me, she rebuked that children frequently misjudged parents, therefore, I should give them a chance. Indeed, we had seen small changes in Pop's line of thinking. Perhaps my teacher was right, besides it did not appear as if there was a choice.

Attempting to make this as smooth as possible, after dinner, I awkwardly prefaced the delicate discussion as a school assignment. Then, I quickly offered recognition that I was too young to date, but perhaps we could apply this concept when I was older. Mom stayed mute while Pop immediately launched into a diatribe about my teacher's motivations, her inappropriate intrusion in family decisions and a few other irrational notions that made it crystal clear nothing had changed. Silently exasperated, I finished washing the dinner dishes and went to my room to finish my homework. Alone, my imagination took me to a place with ordinary parents to complete the questionnaire. The project was graded and returned to me stamped with a happy face and a note: *VERY NICE! Aren't you glad you had this talk with your parents?*

Even with our strict foolish rules, we were never bored and preserved an infinite space of freedom with our extended family. Our revolving door of kin and friends included some from overseas. We met our cousin Paolo and Uncle Franco who visited from Switzerland in the mid-70s. Paolo was sociable, charismatic and free spirited. My friends quickly became his. We spent many late hours with Alfredo, Gino and friends around our kitchen table playing cards or talking through the wee hours of the night.

Some of my friends had boyfriends. Not dating did not mean that I didn't have adolescent crushes. Teenage birthday celebrations for girls involved sleepovers, accordingly, I was always expected to leave before bedtime to sleep in my own bed. I never wholly fit in and finding a balance was not easy.

A spontaneous invitation to visit *Orsara* with my grandparents and my cousin was perfectly timed. That summer would be fabulous and I too would have fun summer experiences to share upon my return to school.

Nonni had pre-arranged for an *Orsaresi* taxi to collect us from Fiumicino Airport in Rome. I was overawed by the magnificent monuments and fountains that I had never seen in any of my previous visits to Italy. As we drove farther south, the Italy from my childhood became more visible by the quaint villages dotting the countryside.

Visits with cousins, aunts, uncles, my maternal grandmother and my godmother whom I had not seen for almost a decade was beyond thrilling. A lot had changed, yet it all looked the same. Some homes had been divided into multiple rooms with a wall separating the bedroom area. Indoor plumbing was common as were indoor toilets and washing machines. Some homes were equipped with a small tank that warmed water for a few hours each day. Every facet of that three week excursion was magnificent, even if I had to explain, once or twice, that I was not in search for a husband. In our culture, it was typical to send girls to our home town when their age was suitable for marriage.

That fabulous adventure to *Orsara* helped me to better appreciate my life in America. It had provided more insight into the sacrifices that my parents had made for us, our little family. Like all girls of my age, I would have liked to fit in better despite my different cultural background. It was during those turbulent moments that I agonized from not being recognized for who I was, not *Orsaresi*, not French and not American, just me.

That trip helped me recognize that I did not need to fit in perfectly in my confusing environment. It was fine to create my own space. What was always firm and without fail, was my family cohesion anyplace that we were together. That was the moment that I had decided that fitting in was far less important than creating my own space in my heart to become the Olga that I wanted to be.

Inevitably, my journey brought back memories for Mom who had not returned to *Orsara* since we had left France. The following summer, she made her way back for six weeks. Even without being told, there was no question that our house had become my responsibility.

I took care of my brothers, Pop and the obvious: meals and cleaning the house. Pop left money for groceries. Lacking a driver's license, sometimes Elisa took us to the store for our weekly shopping. Once, I convinced my brothers to walk with me but carrying all of the grocery bags home, made that mile seem considerably longer. Rightly so, they refused to do it again and wouldn't let me go alone, so we occasionally took a taxi. Pop ordinarily brought home a healthy harvest from the big garden that I could usually figure out how to prepare. No one complained about the dinners until a green bean stew was served for three days in a row. After dinner, Pop calmly threatened to cover my head with it if it appeared again. It was not lost on me that he hated green beans and only ate them under duress.

The house was kept clean but I always waited until everyone was in bed before washing the floor. One night, Pop startled me and ordered me to go to bed. Knowing he had to rise early for work, then go to his second job, I felt awful. When I claimed to be almost finished, he simply took the mop from my hand, sent me to bed and finished my work. That was my last late night project.

With Mom in Italy, there was no one to chase me away from her sewing machine. Our clothes were still predominantly handmade and Mom, still the perfectionist, systematically resewed everything. Our trunk that had once transported our linens from *Fenain*, was in the attic filled with a nice supply of fabric. Thanks to Dominic who managed the cutting department of his cousin's dress factory, we were permitted to periodically rummage their remnant table.

Diving headlong into our crate, my wardrobe was replenished with pants suits, skirts and blazers for the start of high school in the fall. Skirts were preferred over dresses since they rolled up at the waist more easily to convert into a mini skirt upon arriving at school.

At the start of high school, some ancient drama resurfaced. Our paternal nonni had disposed of their property in Italy. Pop was promised a small parcel of land that his parents had chosen to retain a bit longer. During a casual conversation one afternoon, Pop haphazardly discovered that that land had already been disposed of. The broken promise left Pop stunned and deeply hurt. Evidently, even with all of the years gone by, his mother still had not forgiven Pop for defying her to marry my mother. By her standards, Pop should have married up the social ladder. Mom's family had been poorer.

Dinner that evening became leftovers. It was unbearably silent. Upset and scarcely audible, Pop confessed that his intention had been to provide a nest egg for us, his children. We were all heartbroken for him. Almost in unison, each of us, in our own way emphasized that we neither wanted nor needed it. We were rich already, we had each other. The old stuff was just the old stuff. It did not mean to forget…only to keep looking forward. The things he already knew because those were the kinds of things that he had done himself, and the kinds of things that he had often told us. But, his pain was deep and, that day, other bad memories revisited him.

My siblings and I will never forget that day. Spent, Pop and Mom both retired to their bed early. Elisa, Alfredo, Dominic, me and Gino, then twelve, stayed seated at the kitchen table until the wee hours. Our already serious conversations grew more and more profound. We unanimously agreed that it had taken us a long time to be where we were and for the most part, we liked our life. We also acknowledged that even among us, each of us was different. We didn't agree on everything but we always respected each other's ideas. We loved our parents and understood that they had endured and sacrificed a great deal.

That night we made a pact. We promised each other that no matter how different we became or how much we disagreed, we would always respect one another. That did not prevent me from sabotaging the boys' hot water in their showers by running cold water in the kitchen sink when they annoyed me. We still disagreed and argued a lot, but we stayed very close and protected each other unconditionally.

That also did not mean that Pop was less unreasonable about other things. My adolescent years brought to light other unrealistic expectations. In his book of life and in a less than perfect world, a good man provided for his family. As such, investment in a college education seemed to be more important for boys. It did not imply that all boys needed a college education. He respected all who worked hard regardless of what they did. Girls put their intelligence in marrying smart, raising children and enjoying the financial stability provided by their husbands. My thoughts and beliefs were so far removed from my father's that, occasionally, I wondered if they had adopted me. Nevertheless, my focus stayed on my studies without the slighted interest in becoming "that" woman.

In that vein, my curriculum in high school followed the college prep path. I had been accepted in the honors English and history programs. Hands down,

90

my favorite class in high school was English. Our teacher, who was only a few years older than the students, was one of the most interesting and insightful persons that I had ever met. She taught us literary criticism. She showed us how to gain insight into the authors' intentions and how literature mimicked life and humanity. Our deep classroom discussions opened my eyes to some of the problems in the world and significantly helped to shape as well as give direction to my life.

In regards to the honors history class, my real interest was in a three day field trip to Colonial Virginia. Basically, I committed to three years of really hard work for what I saw as my only opportunity to spend a few night away from home. It was far, so it meant overnight stays at a hotel. The trip was not mandatory, but the truth was bent a bit by telling Pop that in order to continue to do well in the program, it was imperative to partake in that excursion. Perplexed that he said yes without hesitation or with his usual million annoying questions, there were no follow up questions on my part, just in case he changed his mind. That outing resulted into a phenomenal life experience. Perhaps it was the experience or perhaps it was the freedom that was desired, either way, I sometimes found myself fantasizing about living in Virginia.

My summers in high school became radically freer as Alfredo and Gino became older. They were very responsible to look after themselves. Like other high school students, I wanted a summer job. Without a driver's license my options were limited. Knowing the factories in our neighborhood were not hiring students, I tackled them anyway, just in case.

Recalling the owner at the pajama factory who really liked Elisa while she was employed there, I name dropped. He not only remembered her, he interviewed me on the spot. He inquired about school and my field of study, all of which I proudly and passionately talked about. I felt convinced that he would offer me a job when he said, "I'm going to do you a great favor." Then, as kindly as Elisa had described him, he gently stated that the best thing he could do for me was to not hire me! He explained that since I was doing well in school that was where I needed to stay. Starting to work in a mill may set a path to spending the rest of my life there and I deserved a chance for a better opportunity. He suggested continuing to work hard in school, ending my job search and enjoying my time as a child. His words hit me like a ton of bricks.

I was mega angry and simply wanted a job. A few days later, with the recommendation of a school friend, the home for the elderly nearby offered me work in their kitchen. For the duration of my high school years, my job was to set up the trays, deliver them to the residents, then collect and wash them. The work was part time over the summers and on weekends during the school year.

Also during my high school years, Dominic and Elisa had two daughters, Jennifer and Jacelyn who were just under three years apart. They were the light of everyone's heart. I loved being Aunt Olga and my little brothers took their role as uncles to heart. More often than not, one of them was clinging to uncle Gino's leg to prevent him from leaving because they were having too much fun.

The girls equally adored Nana and Popop, as they called my parents. They, in turn, were over the moon in their new role as grandparents. Being more settled at that point in their lives, they took the time to simply enjoy their grandchildren. Pop relaxed more and worried less about taking care of us. The sparkle in his eyes returned and his softer personality reemerged. Both Elisa and Dominic encouraged their children to partake in activities. The girls began dancing very young and every performance was a family affair!

We were all thrilled that our parents had that opportunity for a new chapter in their lives.

Most of my free time was spent with Jennifer and Jacelyn, at their house or ours. My sister's home was still the only place that I was permitted to sleep over, but my driver's license allowed me the freedom to visit them anytime.

Getting my license had been delayed for as long as possible because in my mind, it only meant more responsibility at home and not enough time to devote to my studies. College had always felt like a dream that seemed impossibly out of reach and ridiculous to expect. In reality, it was never a topic of conversation so I was neither encouraged nor prohibited. My belief was that although we were very comfortable as a family at that point, I didn't think that we had the money to spend on that, so the question was never asked.

I'd had some exposure to a university nearby during my time in high school. Having exhausted the foreign language opportunities for French in high school, I was permitted to enroll in French courses at Moravian College. I loved everything about the campus and the college atmosphere. It was not a state college so it wasn't an option for me but, just in case a miracle happened, I petitioned for my American Citizenship in order to apply for college loans for an in-state school.

Time passed and my high school graduation approached. Since my desire to attend college still had not been shared with anyone, that door closed. Having supplemented my curriculum with a few business classes, just in case, lessened my worries.

A week prior to graduation, I interviewed for my first professional job, a receptionist in a small social service agency. It was scheduled for early morning since it was a school day. Choosing to walk the two miles to think combined with an incredibly hot day determined my attire: shorts, t-shirt and sandals.

Upon entering the reception area, my lack of preparedness for that interview became abundantly clear. Too late to worry about my appearance, I sat, grabbed my notes, and focused on cramming for final exams.

Surprisingly, the Executive Director telephoned a few days later with a job offer. Excited for an opportunity in a professional job, my only question was in regards to the start date. He paused, then asked if I wished to hear the salary before accepting. It never occurred to me that salaries were negotiable. Embarrassed, I only expressed my confidence that whatever he decided would be fair.

While sharing the news with Elisa, she reminded me of the other offer for full-time employment from the home for the elderly. That one came with a raise. After doing the math, it resulted in an increase of ten cents per hour versus the flat salary offered at the social service agency. Although, I heard what she was saying, the words of the owner at the pajama factory echoed much louder in my head. My decision had been made.

Graduating alongside my classmates with the bi-centennial class of 1976 was bittersweet. My entire family was present at the ceremony that was held in the school gym. They proudly stood and applauded each time they heard my name alongside various distinctions for achievements in both academic and business paths.

The week prior to starting my new job, I had eagerly sewn myself some new clothes. Although my attire was appropriate for my position, my professional wardrobe was still fairly sparse. Elisa had also taken me on a surprise shopping spree at Orr's, a little boutique in downtown Bethlehem. It was on the pricy side, but we combed the sale rack and she bought me five new dresses to wear to work.

My first week in the workforce with the not-for-profit organization that provided services to blind and visually impaired individuals, was far from typical. Interviews related to a sexual harassment investigation were underway. While merely observing in the periphery, that incident opened my eyes to some harsh realities and challenges for women in the workplace.

The staff of approximately five was very kind to me. My job, on the other hand, was not challenging or stimulating. Bored to tears within the first few weeks, my pleas for additional work were answered with more stacks of paper to file. Craving some challenging projects, my attention turned to the company financials, however, my boss claimed that work was too hard and too important. With some persistence, he either agreed or gave up and took the time to train me to do that work. Within a month, there was no shortage of real work. He had handed off all of the work associated with the financials and payroll.

By fall, a staffing shortage to conduct their preschool vision screenings allowed me to assist with that too. When the company needed a notary on staff, I offered to apply. That function was especially useful in my personal life. We had numerous documents that needed to be notarized to sponsor family migrating to America. Eventually, there was more work than time, which was an arrangement that suited me well.

Soon after the Executive Director resigned around 1978, the president of the board of directors called me to schedule time in the office. He wanted to take care of the financials until a new director was hired. Confused, I informed him that the books were balanced, invoices and payroll were completed and the checks were ready for his signature. We were both taken aback. Evidently, the board members were unaware that work had been handed off to me several years prior. Barely twenty-one years old and the youngest person on staff, I had always been highly regarded within the company but, in that moment, losing the most interesting part of my job was worrisome. To my relief, he advised me to continue doing that work as well as managing the office until the director position was filled.

Regrettably, I had mistakenly interpreted that to mean that I was a qualified candidate to fill the director position. To my disappointment, my resume was not even considered. The president of the board made a personal visit to kindly explain that the position required a college degree. He thanked me for all my work during the transition and, as a valued employee, the board of directors hoped that the event would not cause me to leave the company. The dagger sank in a little deeper in my heart, accentuating my idea to advance without a degree was not going to work well.

Despite my wallowing, the new director was amazing and my work progressed. Her main focus was on writing proposals for some desperately needed new programs at the agency. The full financial workload remained my responsibility. She promoted me to office manager and authorized me to hire two people: a receptionist and another to conduct the preschool vision screening as that program was also expanding. That evolution also came with a huge raise.

Life at home did not vary. Alfredo and Gino were doing very well in school. Their games in our back alley had moved to the community playground nearby, but the kids continued to routinely congregate on our front porch. Around Halloween, some of the neighborhood teenagers tick-tacked homes. It was an irritating prank by boys who threw corn against the front door then ran off. The ticking noise was annoying but benign.

Occasionally, more mischievous kids threw rotten tomatoes or eggs which were utterly disgusting to clean up. Obviously Pop found this extremely disrespectful. They had picked the wrong house to tick-tack. Knowing the kids in the neighborhood, he thought he had a pretty good idea of who the culprits were, but the boys ran too fast for him.

After removing egg slime from the front door a few times, Pop was livid and even more determined to deal with that situation. Strategically positioning himself near the front door, the first sound of ticking allowed him to quickly bolt out the door. Flying over the five steps off the porch, he caught a glimpse of one of the boys he thought he had recognized and stayed on his tail until he ran out of steam. Breathless, Pop had no choice but to stop.

By chance, Alfredo, who had been out on a date, noticed Pop on the sidewalk almost three miles from our home. Puzzled to see him there, he stopped. Pop climbed into the pickup truck huffing and puffing. Alfredo glimpsed at Pop's feet which were covered with only remnants of sock threads. No words were exchanged until after Alfredo dropped off his date, then he asked if Pop was OK. Very unconvincingly, Pop, who was still catching his breath, replied, "I almost getta...."

Pop had never laid a hand on any child so we were not sure what he would have done if he had caught him. We were not too worried about that. In the end, Pop wore shoes the next time he positioned himself by the front door but the tick-tacking had miraculously stopped. It took weeks before the alleged culprit attempted to re-enter our home. No words regarding the incident were exchanged. We noticed more and more that Pop's bark was probably worse than his bite.

Alfredo was next to graduate from high school. He was bright, quiet and sociable. He loved to play soccer and hockey, but his passion was basketball. He also always had an appetite for nice cars. He typically drove Pop's half-ton pick-up truck to school while the car was reserved for me to drive to work, unless he conned me into switching with him because it was way cooler to have his girlfriend ride in the car. He also worked part time preparing and delivering meals to the elderly. After high school, he began his college education at Penn State University.

It was Gino's turn to enter high school. He was smart, funny and more adventurous and rebellious than the rest of us. While in high school, he worked part time in various local restaurants at walking distance. With his earnings, he purchased his first used car at the age of sixteen. Interestingly, on Gino's first lesson in the Two Guys parking lot, it was clear to Pop that he did not need guidance.

A few colorful words escaped between Pop's breaths. Gino cautiously asked what to do next. In his broken English, Pop muttered, "We go ome." So Gino drove them home. Mom had been eager to hear about Gino's progress, whereas

Gino smartly remained silent giving Pop time to answer. Pop, looked over the top of his glasses and simply said, "He know to drive …Tomorrow we get license."

Gino stayed busy and active. He joined a roller skating dancing team that performed under the strobe lights throughout the evening. He tried teaching me to skate, but still being severely uncoordinated, it was hopeless.

Gino also liked to tinker with old cars and sometimes soup them up a bit. He also loved motorcycles and dirt bikes. On a whim, sitting around bored one day, he and his friend decided they needed a Honda three-wheeler. Even though Pop paid for the bike, he was baffled by this desire. He asked what he could possibly need with that frivolous three-wheeler. Gino loved to push Pop's buttons, the bike was the opportunity and the response. It did come in handy during a heavy snow storm as the front page of a local newspaper had reported. Gino, his friend and their bikes were pretty much the only ones able to get around our neighborhood. They spent the entire day transporting neighbors who were stranded, to and from work at the hospital or at the home for the elderly nearby.

Occasionally, my work involved partaking in community events where I met an incredible friend. He was male, so unless I was prepared for some drama with Pop, dating him was not an option…at least that was my assumption. Quite frankly, even the thought of trying to explain our "francoameritalian" culture to an unfamiliar American seemed absurd. Instead, I treated this relationship delicately by telling my siblings and staying tightlipped with my parents.

We bonded instantly. He helped me to grow more spiritually and to accept that it was not wrong to be a little selfish to want things for myself. Yet, in an odd way, I felt even more trapped. Finding that balance on my own path while honoring family duty seemed impossible. Furthermore, keeping a relationship secret was too complicated. It weighed too heavily on me so I ended it.

My sister had married at the age twenty-one and was still happily in her relationship now seven years later. Married or not, my life was different than hers. My first time bringing a guy home had been someone that I had known well since grade school. As a result, I comfortably prepped my date on what to expect from Pop, and even provided him a few tips on responses, just to get through it.

The joke was on me. The embarrassing conversation with my friend was all for not. Perhaps Pop's thinking had changed because he was not even home.

In truth, it was not a boyfriend that I was seeking, it was simply a bit more independence. In that vein, knowing my aspiration of moving into the city, Alfredo had given me a tip about a vacant apartment. The outcome was completely disastrous. That concept was still foreign for Pop. The subject of one of his daughters leaving the family cocoon to settle alone in the city before getting married was still unthinkable. Mom was useless with any intervention. Elisa, as always, came to my defense but also complicated the situation. After offering to look at the apartment with me, she quickly pointed out all of the reasons for not residing in that place. I was keenly aware that the apartment was not even remotely nice, but where she saw problems, I saw independence. Even if it had been perfect, she would have persuaded me that home was better.

Despite her good intentions to keep me safe, she made me feel guilty. She did not understand what I was looking for. Perhaps I didn't understand it myself. Without my family, my independence meant nothing. There had to be a way to have both without feeling guilty.

During a tirade with my "big brother" concerning my intense discontent with where my life was headed, the idea of moving away instead of moving out simply rolled from my lips. Tired of hearing that reoccurring theme, Dominic finally blurted, "Just do it. I agree with you. You have two choices: stop talking about it or do something. It's up to you. Just know that I will always be there for you." Shocked and relieved to hear those words, there was no doubt that he understood. Moreover, it provided the affirmation deeply needed to put some distance between me and my existing life. Still, it terrified me.

First and foremost was to secure a new job. In the months that followed, I arranged a visit to Virginia, a state in the southern part of the country where some of my high school friends had found employment after their college graduation. The drive there was approximately four hours plus another hour making a few wrong turns. One entire day was spent riding the subway to various businesses in Northern Virginia and Washington, D.C. dropping off resumes. Relying on walk-ins since future appointments were problematic with a few days stay in town, I let my feet burn to a myriad of companies that had posted ads in the newspaper. Only one interview had been pre-scheduled for the end of the day with the same company where my friend worked.

Oblivious to the weather forecast, I had neither raincoat nor umbrella to protect me from the downpour. Additionally, my arms were full of gifts for my nieces that had been accumulated between subway stops. Everything from head to toe was completely soaked by the time I reached my interview. Even though the situation continued to deteriorate, rescheduling was not an option for me.

Upon entering the lobby, my waterlogged bag disintegrated, scattering my souvenirs all over the floor. The gentlemen who planned to conduct the first part of the interview helped to collect and transfer my gifts into a plastic bag. A good first impression was completely out of the window. At that point, being sheltered from the pouring rain and off my aching feet had to be sufficient. Heels had not been a good choice either. Then again, stretching to four foot eleven inches, they had become an indispensable necessity. The second portion of the interview conducted by the manager, a three-star general, lasted nearly three hours. We chatted a little about the job, then moved on to life, family, Italy and France.

Hopeful for a job offer, upon my return home it seemed wise to alert my family, specifically Pop. Counting on his deep respect for hard work and improving oneself, I confessed the obvious. Marriage was not part of my dream. My focus was exclusively on my career. The conversation stayed very light with few words exchanged. That day, so many different emotions flooded through me. A part of me was also deeply conflicted about leaving my brothers. Alfredo was in college whereas Gino was younger. I still felt responsible for him. Each time the telephone rang, my heart skipped a beat. When the call arrived, my decision was made only when the words drifted from my lips.

With that, my world was going to change again. Announcing the acceptance to my family, my eyes stayed fixed on Pop. In the softest voice, he asked if my decision was certain. Confirming, his eyes revealed both pride and fear. It was what I felt too. Without hesitation, he agreed that it sounded like a great opportunity. For me, giving him a reasonable justification for his daughter to leave home was a huge relief. His concern over our family going in different directions was much easier to address. I reassured him that as crazy as they were, abandoning them was simply impossible.

Gathering documents necessary for the start of my new job, Pop directed me to the drawer with all of our important papers in the master bedroom. There, my eyes stumbled upon several thick manila envelopes, each holding our names. Too curious to think about it for more than a second, I peeked inside the sleeve that held my name. Inside, there were years of report cards, newspaper clippings with honor roll mentions and articles of recognition for my volunteer work for the American Cancer Society. Pop had even highlighted the distinctions on my graduation bulletin. For all of this time that I thought he was not paying attention, he had not missed anything.

A succession of bittersweet get-togethers with friends and co-workers mixed in with the Christmas celebrations concluded 1980. A few days later, my parents and brothers moved me into my tiny sixth floor apartment in Virginia.

Adapting to my new environment was harder than I had ever imagined. Managing my money was the easy part. My earnings paid my bills first, then I ate. My budget always included sufficient money for weekly toll calls to my family. What was unbearable was the loneliness. I profoundly missed the day-to-day interaction with them. Although they visited often, sometimes it took all of my strength not to pack up and go home.

Sometimes my parents surprised me by bringing my nieces whom I deeply missed. Phone call rituals always included heart-to-hearts with my girls. Jennifer hurried to the phone. On the flipside, Jacelyn was a little cooler with the initial calls. Then four-year-old Jacelyn sounded in the distance, "If Aunt Olga wants to talk to me, she can come home." Accordingly, the eight hour round trip home at least once per month became routine.

A year later Alfredo married Cheryle. The lovebirds had met while working a summer job at a restaurant. Both had decided to take a break from college to start their life together. Four years later, their son, Michael, was born. He was a charming and spunky little man with an abundance of energy. Jennifer, Jacelyn and Michael grew up together as our home easily transformed into the grandchildren's second home. To say that I didn't immensely miss being part of that life would be a lie.

Life, on my own, was radically different from our family filled get-togethers and the front porch gatherings. A second job at the jewelry counter of a retail store lessened some of the loneliness. It also assisted in paying off my car loan early since being in debt brought more anxiety. There, I met my life-long friend, Rogena. She worked the second job to put herself through law school. Rogena was incredibly intelligent. She was one of the most grounded, independent and determined women I had ever met. Our cultures and where we were in life varied while our goals were similar and the connections to our respective families were equally strong.

As the years passed, we never allowed the distance to separate us. It was common for me to bring friends home, especially around the holidays if they did not have family nearby. My family especially adored Rogena. Upon meeting them, she confessed that entering the home of my parents was like stepping into a very old Italian film. When my parents visited, she often joined us for dinner but needed to first clear her entire day because it was not uncommon for Rogena and Pop to huddle at the kitchen table for hours chatting about everything and nothing.

In my heart, there were no regrets that my decision had been right for me. Although the differences between social services and that of a contractor on a military defense project was drastic, I adapted to my new life and my job. Romanticizing my time as an independent Mary Richards[22] was easy. For some of the more difficult times, I convinced myself that whatever my feelings and needs, they paled in comparison to the hardships my parents had endured. If

---

[22] Mary Richards: Character on a television series, The *Mary Tyler Moore Show*. A sitcom that aired from September 19, 1970 through March 19, 1977.

they overcame theirs, I was determined to overcome mine. With that, I moved forward with conviction.

7

Just married

By my mid-twenties, I made two major decisions. One in my career, the other in my personal life. As my job had substantially evolved, it inspired me to consider a different career future, one that necessitated a degree in a technical domain. As the years had passed, my desire to go to college had been overshadowed by the lapse in time, affordability and a busy full-time job. It was with the encouragement from Susan, the best boss that I have ever had, that I enrolled at the community college. The company's Continuing Education Program assisted in defraying the cost of my classes provided the courses were within a range of their pre-defined technical fields.

My prior vision of a degree in foreign languages was no longer an option, conversely, it was more aligned with my professional life. As my studies progressed, Susan's infinite support was demonstrated by offering me more and more challenging work to show me the possibilities to grow in my job.

At the same time, my biological clock was ticking. Wanting children without nuptials on the horizon was complicated. I was also deeply grateful that my parents never even hinted about the whys or why nots of marriage. Nevertheless, my effort to adopt as a single parent was complicated and unproductive. Eligibility required more financial stability than my present state of affairs.

That prompted me to establish myself as a homeowner which avoided wasting a lot of money in rent. Since property was very expensive closer to the city, it forced me to look for a more affordable home farther out than I would have liked. The three-bedroom, three level end-unit townhouse made my commute to work in Washington, D.C. well over an hour each way.

A settlement scheduled on the day before Thanksgiving made it impossible to spend that holiday with my family. Instead, it was spent locally with my dear friend Rogena and her family.

Soon after the holiday, my parents rented a truck to transport most of my furniture that had been temporarily stored at their home. When the truck arrived, the house felt more like my home. Mom and Pop stayed for a few days to help me get organized. Pop, who never liked being idle, had brought his own tools with him, just in case. He went to Lowes to buy lumber and plywood. By the time I returned very late after work and classes, Pop had proudly finished paneling my laundry room and organized it.

Without a car, they needed me to drive them back home, an eight-hour round trip. Final exams were scheduled around the same time. I jokingly asked my friend and co-worker, John, if he was up to a one-day road trip to drive my parents back to Pennsylvania. Completely unanticipated, he replied with a serious, "Sure. I have no plans for Saturday."

John and I had known each other for over a year in our jobs dealing with a consulting project for the government that was modernizing the system for air traffic control. He was an engineer, I was involved in configuration management. In my position, I interacted with almost everyone inside and outside of my company, at all levels. It was a huge project with an office filled with young people with whom we formed close bonds.

Together, we participated in a myriad of cultural and social events. One of the most pleasurable was the company sponsored softball team that John and I had both joined. We were matched against other consulting companies involved with the same government contract. We played weekly in spring and fall on the greens of the Washington D.C. Mall all bordered by the Smithsonian museums. We brought our own equipment: bats, gloves, bases and coolers full of beer and water. Invariably, I was the worst player on the team. Enlisting me had nothing to do with my athletic capabilities. Each team was required to have at least four women on their roster. It was a blast. After our games, the teams all congregated for happy hour and dancing at the Warehouse, a small bar across the street from where we worked.

When the day arrived to return my parents to Fountain Hill, we picked John up en route early in the morning. It was the first time they had met one another. Pop skootched to the back seat with Mom while John hopped in the front of my two door Plymouth. It was a reasonably enjoyable drive, with the exception of Pop who was relentless about my heavy foot. I knew that ignoring him was a huge mistake even before the flashing lights appeared in my rearview mirror about halfway home.

Immediately after pulling over, Pop tapped my shoulder. It was his cue to go outside for a smoke, another huge source of irritation with me. We blamed the smoking for his cough that was becoming progressively hoarser. We had all begged him to quit, but he was not interested in our opinions when it came to cigarettes. He simply disregarded our pleas. My counterattack was to ignore him during my exchange with the police officer. Really wanting out, he proceeded by tapping John's shoulder. As the officer handed me my first speeding ticket, under my breath, I whispered to John not to let Pop out. John, very confused by the entire interaction, simply pretended not to notice Pop or my ticket. Pop was left trapped in the car without a smoke.

When we arrived at my sister's home, the table was already prepared for a feast. With the exception of Alfredo, who was busy with work, the entire family was already present. It was customary that on my visits home, we all gathered together. Though that visit was for only a few hours, it was no different. My niece, Jacelyn, who was still in the shower, grabbed a towel when she heard my voice and ran so fast, she left a trail of dripping water all the way into the kitchen. John, a little overwhelmed but flexible and sociable enough, had no difficulty to find his place in my very awkward family. On our return trip, we took a small detour at the restaurant where Alfredo worked because I didn't want to leave without saying hello and hugging him too.

The four hour road trip to Virginia passed quickly. John drove, I talked. We had already connected on an intellectual level. During that trip, we opened up more about ourselves. Our talks had always felt natural and easy. We had always been honest with one another and neither of us ever felt the need to be someone that we were not. Our core values and backgrounds were similar. We talked about many things. Mostly, I advised him on reconciling with the girlfriend that he had recently broken up with.

A few days later, as promised for his help with the driving, we had dinner at a Chinese restaurant and saw the new Star Trek IV movie, *The Voyage Home* at the theatre. Perhaps a bit cliché, but this was the beginning to our own voyage home because from that day forward, we were inseparable. From John's first encounter with my family, he embraced their authenticity and the richness of our culture. With that, he fully accepted me.

John's family was from West Virginia, in a place with a similar socioeconomic background as ours. The state, very mountainous with beautiful rolling hills in the middle of the Appalachian region, was rich in logging and coal. Although farming was limited because of its mountainous terrain, both of John's parents had grown up on a farm during the Great Depression.

His mother, Helen Kimble Waters, the youngest of six was born in 1921. She lost her mother to illness at the age of thirteen. Her oldest sister, Mary, was married and well-settled. Her husband was fortunate to have a well-paid job, a rarity for such a poor place during the depression. Accordingly, when Helen grew up, Mary paid for her studies at the Business College so she would have better employment opportunities. Those studies offered Helen an excellent position at the West Virginia University as the administrative assistant for the Athletic Department.

John's dad, William Donald (Don) Waters, was born in 1912. He was the eldest of two boys. Hopeful for better work opportunities, he applied to the university in Morgantown, the closest in proximity. After one semester at the West Virginia University, he was forced to drop out. Not only was the college far, transportation was not easily accessible. He walked for several miles before even reaching the bus stop that took him the rest of the way to his campus. The commute imposed huge time constraints that severely interfered with his family chores on the farm.

Soon after, Don enlisted in the Air Force during WWII. He was stationed in Australia and the Philippines where he prepared and coordinated requisitions forms, a position affording him less exposure than other soldiers. Upon his return from the military, he worked at the Olin Mathieson Chemical plant that had been built during WWII, in part, to create deuterium oxide, an essential element used to manufacture the atomic bomb.

John's parents had known each other before Don left for the military, but their relationship had been brief and platonic. Letters had never been exchanged. When he returned from the service, they met again by chance. During their brief encounter, he noted her telephone number. By the time she returned from her lunch break, the phone on her desk was already ringing. They married shortly after and had two handsome boys, Bill in 1950 and John in 1955.

Growing up, John always had cats and dogs. He loved all animals and he adored the outdoors. His childhood home was situated on three acres full of beautiful trees and a small pond in Harmony Grove, a rural community outside of Morgantown. John's grandparents had purchased that land many years prior from the parents of Don Knotts, the actor who played Barney Fife on the 1960 sitcom, *The Andy Griffith Show*.

While the children were still very young, the chemical plant closed and left Don unemployed. John's mother, Helen, was forced to return to work at the University of West Virginia in the Physical Education Department where she stayed for the next twenty years. Don was soon hired by a bank in Morgantown where he too worked for over twenty years. Having grown up in the Great Depression, they were very frugal. In his free time, Don cultivated a vegetable garden while Helen canned almost everything. Her specialty was strawberry rhubarb jam.

It was hard to believe that one room school houses still existed during that time, but that was where John attended elementary school. When the school closed shortly before the start of sixth grade, the students were bussed to a larger elementary school near Morgantown.

John stayed busy mostly outdoors and was always involved in projects of sorts. His mother often asked him why he returned home so dirty. He replied very simply, "Because I do things." At the age of seven, he had created a newsletter for his neighborhood. He interviewed neighbors and reported on community events. Their forest fire where firefighters had to intervene was a special event that he reported on. His dry sense of humor was revealed even at a very young age in the "Joke Column" of his newsletter. His mother typed his circular for which he charged five cents per issue.

When John turned twelve, the state considered building a major highway that forced his family to sell their precious property. In exchange, they were made a ridiculous offer obliging them to buy a smaller, more expensive house near the city of Morgantown.

At the Waters household, gatherings were central to their family cohesion. Annual family vacations took them to the beaches of Ocean City Maryland, Don's favorite place. On May 30, they piled in several cars that followed one another toward the cemetery in Davis, West Virginia, Helen's birthplace, to pay their respects to Helen's baby sister and her mother's gravesites. Afterwards, the extended family picnicked all together in Blackwater Falls near the Canaan Valley. Since that area was often still very cold during that time of year, it was not uncommon to grill their food while wearing gloves.

Helen and Don encouraged their boys to get involved in activities. In high school, John played the trombone in their marching and symphonic bands. They played at halftime for football games. Occasionally, they travelled to large cities such as New York City or Indianapolis to partake in parades.

John always worked at one odd job or another. While in high school, he worked part time in the clubhouse at the golf course.

At sixteen, he purchased his first car for $150 from his brother who had been drafted in the Army. The used 1964 Kadett Opel needed an enormous amount of repairs. Having limited funds, John quickly learned to do the upkeep himself.

In 1974, John was accepted at the West Virginia University in their College of Engineering. The lack of money did not permit him to live on campus. Oftentimes, he lunched at his Aunt Mary's who lived nearby. She was a football fan, better yet, she served beer and pizza. Every college student's dream! During his college years, John worked at the university golf course and other odd jobs to pay for his education. Over the course of a few summers, he worked in Ocean City at various upscale restaurants. Still without a reliable car, his mother often recalled a certain occasion with car parts spread out all over the driveway while John had left to cover his local part-time job. She was not sure what miracle had occurred, but she was immensely impressed by her son's improvisational auto-mechanic abilities. John had managed to put his car back together, then drove the seven hours to the beach that same night to start his summer job the following morning.

After a few semesters, time and money had interfered with his university studies. John dropped out to work full time. He returned a year later transferring from engineering to business. Another year had passed before he realized that discipline did not interest him. Reassessing his career plan, John redirected himself to the engineering domain which required him to retake some classes since he had been away from it for too long. Money and time were of the essence. Accordingly, he relearned many of the pre-requisites on his own in order to avoid the cost of retaking classes. Despite that, John always made time for fun on the ski slopes.

During his final days at the university, John attended their annual Job Fair. He received two offers from the Department of Navy. He accepted the job in their Electronic Division to work on radio communications for naval ships which better aligned with his field of study. The position was in Arlington, Virginia, where he moved across the street from my apartment in 1981. It was several moves and several jobs later for each of us before we met while working for the same company five years later.

Soon after we began to date, I met his parents over dinner at a Mexican restaurant, El Bandidos. About a month later, John's father suffered a fatal heart attack. I met the extended family at Don's funeral in West Virginia. Even under those difficult circumstances, they were very welcoming and immediately accepted me as a part of their family. Upon meeting Aunt Mary, she quizzed me on my knowledge of football. Growing up in a university town, essentially all family members were devoted fans of the WVU football team, most had season tickets. There was no faking it on my part, I replied honestly, "I don't follow football." She declared that could pose a problem for us. After reassuring her that I was a fast learner, we both laughed and hugged.

Our future family visits were always together. Pop taught John to play Pinochle so he joined in the after dinner games with Dominic, Alfredo and Gino. Aunt Mary and John's mom offered us their tickets to the university football games. My knowledge of the sport had not improved, but I loved going to the games. Undoubtedly, Aunt Mary had forgiven me because we saw her often and she was always delighted with our get-togethers.

While John and I were very different, we were in-sync about the things that were important to us. For the most obvious difference, John was just over six feet tall while I had to stretch to reach four feet eleven inches. He had a great sense of humor, a bit dry. He was kind, soft spoken and talked far less than me. He avoided obstacles while I dealt with them head on. I analyzed and wanted to talk about things while he waited to see how they worked out. I made him a little crazier while he kept me a little calmer.

As John was not very talkative, he also did not toss sweet nothings frivolously although, from time to time, he did surprise me. Recalling a comical occasion, I had asked when he knew that he loved me. We both had to laugh at his, "I knew you were the one when you were throwing up over the side of Dan's boat just before the big race." John and Dan raced sailboats together. Never having sailed mixed with a bit of motion sickness, hadn't deterred me from trying. Why not? For that memorable race, we had both partaken in too much happy hour the evening prior. Honestly, I cannot even recall if we won the race that day, but I was invited to return. Eventually, I grew more accustomed to the boat but like all other sports in my life, it was not my thing.

There were many reason why I fell in love with John, then again, he had wholly conquered my heart with his reaction to some unexpected and devastating news. It was unlikely that I would be able to have children and I simply could not imagine my life without them. His first words were, "It's OK. I would like for us to have our own children too, but there are a lot of children in the world that need homes. We can adopt."

Our families were thrilled to learn we decided to marry in autumn. As appearances were never a concern for me, our wedding day was no exception. That morning, I canceled my hair and manicure appointments. The commute to the salon was too far away, besides I preferred to spend the time with my family who had arrived two days prior. My nieces beautified my nails and my sister assisted with my hair. After getting dressed, I felt like a princess in my gorgeous gown and veil that Mom and Elisa had helped me to choose.

At the church, Pop had been waiting for me in the vestibule at the top of the stairs. Finding ourselves alone, face to face and glassy eyed, he gave me his crooked smile with his head cocked slightly to the left, winked and pulled me into his arms. No words were needed. His eyes told me everything will be OK and I am very proud of you while mine said, thank you and sorry for all the troubles. With one last hug, arm-in-arm we entered the small church that illuminated with smiles on the faces of our family and friends. Standing at the altar was my striking future husband in his tuxedo, teal bow-tie and cummerbund.

John declared our wedding reception one of the best parties he had ever been to. It was simple and graced with the company of our families and friends. In honor of this union, we set one very long table for the reception party bonding both of our families together. Our nephew, Michael, also left his imprint on that day. Five years old at that time and bursting with energy, he had decreed himself as our greeter. He stood in the reception area, welcomed our guests and offered them "free" cookies. There was no wedding without Italian cookies, accordingly, my family brought them from an Italian store in Pennsylvania. Michael was simply ensuring that they were getting their proper attention.

John did a great job of hiding his Honda Prelude from pranksters, namely Gino and John's brother who were on the prowl. They were unsuccessful in finding the car but when we left, our lengthy Italian goodbyes allowed them plenty of time for their attack. Hideous strings of cans were mysteriously attached to our bumper during the "congratulations" and "we love yous." The ruckus that ensued as we drove away triggered howls of kings by Gino and all of his accomplices behind us. John and I rolled our eyes then laughed all the way to the hotel.

One of the conspirators was Rogena who had given us a small box and took a peculiarly long time to stress opening it as soon as we arrived at the hotel. It was another surprise. She had cancelled our existing reservation. The box held a key to the bridal suite that she had booked for us instead.

Our honeymoon in Barbados marked John's first time out of the country. Despite the intermittent downpours over the course of that week, it was incredibly beautiful. Its sunsets were spectacular. Breakfast was served on the veranda overlooking the ocean. The birds adored this view too, well they mostly loved the breakfast buffet at their disposal. We had to battle them to keep ours each morning. Outnumbered, one bird superbly dove inside my glass of orange juice while the attendant nearby gave us the, "I warned you" smile.

As newlyweds and thereafter, our frequent visits to and from Pennsylvania and West Virginia did not vary. We agreed to alternate the major holidays of Christmas and Thanksgiving each year. Both John's family and mine lived four hours away by car in opposing directions.

John's family was kind and warm, and while the concept of splitting the holidays was our idea, it was still enormously difficult. My first Christmas away from my family was profoundly hard. Since we would also not be in our own home for the holidays, John and I had agreed that we would not trim a tree. Sensing my anxiety as the holidays approached, John surprised me with one anyway. I immediately fell in love with its smell and its imperfect shape. Trimming it was a fabulous distraction! Since John did not like flashing lights, it was trimmed in non-blinking white lights and bright red apples. It was simple, crooked and perfect.

What was not at all perfect or amusing was our time-consuming commute to work in Washington, D.C. that had become far too routine for us. We left at 5:30 in the morning to arrive at work by 7:00 AM. We returned home around 7:00 in the evening or later if we played softball or I had classes. There was no time for anything else on weekdays.

On weekends we sailed with Dan, played racquetball at the recreation center nearby, spent time with friends, worked on home projects or we played cards. Other than Pinochle or Black Jack, many American card games were foreign to me, so one night, John taught me to play Rummy. Surely, some great cards had been dealt my way, I kept winning. Then, he taught me to play Hearts. Again, I was winning. That night, John's competitiveness was becoming more and more apparent. To his credit, he did not attempt to change the rules. Nevertheless, it was certain we were never going to bed if he didn't win. So, around two in the morning, tired, I let him win!

My studies not only took up a large chunk of my time but John's too. Going to the university part time became increasingly concerning, it would take forever to finish the program. John understood how important it was to me and always encouraged me to keep going. As a solution, he took a few computer programming classes on the same nights. John also suggested buying a computer to reduce our time in the campus lab. It was our first major investment.

John and I easily fell into married life. We were blissfully happy and comfortable together.

Life…made in the USA

Our married life had changed in the best way imaginable when Danielle arrived in May 1988. My eyes never separated from her own while hers were vivaciously captivated by her new world. A nurse swaddled her in a soft white and pink blanket before resting the pure love in my waiting arms. My emotions were overflowing. An incredible strength was born inside of me ready to embark on a new path full of surprises. Sitting beside my bed, a father was wholly mesmerized at the sight of his daughter. Observing them in that moment made it abundantly clear that John was the one that I wanted to share this fantastic journey with.

Mom and Pop, always thrilled to welcome new arrivals, met their fourth grandchild when we were discharged from the hospital. Mom stayed for the week helping me to get on my feet while Pop returned to his job after a few days. Luckily, Pop's attention was solely on the newborn giving no hint of being angry with me. I had shamelessly taken full advantage of our situation to tell Pop that he could not smoke in our house or around our baby. Ok, not that daring, Mom was recruited to break it to him before they arrived. Although he smoked considerably less, his cough had worsened dramatically. According to Mom, my request infuriated him. Nevertheless, somewhere en route to our house, he rolled down the car window then tossed his entire pack of Camel non-filters across the interstate. He never said a word about it, then or later. Better yet, he never smoked again.

As we began our new family life together, we had agreed unequivocally on having a work-life balance. Devoid of a surplus of funds, a few sacrifices had allowed us to comfortably make those types of choices. Our biggest obstacle, the long weekday commute, was shortened considerably by moving into a much smaller home closer to work before Danielle was three months old. My workweek was also shortened to three days allowing me to spend my days off with our daughter and my evenings at the university.

Raising a child in the "right" way had always worried me. Growing up, our responsibilities had been enormous, especially around caring for our younger siblings. We had been children who took care of children. John on the other hand, had zero experience with young children. To that end, we did the things we thought were right. When life happened, like everyone else, we figured out the rest and hoped not to make too many of our own mistakes along the way.

From her earliest days, Danielle was determined and independent. She taught us "thumbie," by rubbing our thumbnail to soothe herself while reading each night before bed. If crawling did not get her to her destination, she climbed on a little horse that was always on hand nearby. A favored pastime that supplied an entire evening of entertainment involved stacking diapers or rolls of toilet paper on my lap. Dolls were mostly ignored, oftentimes they never came out of their boxes. The only exception was a Weeble doll who aided her to master walking at eleven months. With one doll in her mouth and one in each hand for balance, she walked up and down the kitchen floor. When she fell, she got herself up, placed the tiny dolls in their proper places, and tried again.

Days after becoming more proficient in her new mode of transportation, we journeyed to our favorite place, the National Zoo. In line with her customary response from a book, *Hey, I'm a big girl now*,[23] she rejected her stroller in favor of walking for the entire afternoon. My effort to fix a quick dinner of pasta and peas upon returning home failed miserably. We had placed her dinner on the tray of her high chair. Before returning with our own plates, she was already slouched over the side of her chair, fast asleep. Between two tiny fingers was a green pea that never found its way into her mouth.

After being told that it was unlikely to ever carry a child of my own, to welcoming our second nearly three years later, on Mom's birthday, was beyond bliss! Danielle, who had insisted on a big sister, was over the moon. She instantly took Joel under her protective wing when he arrived.

Joel was beautiful with the longest eyelashes that accentuated his gorgeous eyes. He liked to be rocked but when it came to bedtime, he favored sleeping in his own space, in the crib. With Joel, we learned to do many things with only one arm. He loved to be carried everywhere and anywhere, mostly by me. His right cheek took its place pressed against my left cheek so we were facing the same direction. When we were not cheek-to-cheek, he was most likely disassembling something. The electronic toys such as his ABC table intended to help him learn shapes and letters were upside down, in parts on the floor.

---

[23] *Hey! I'm a big girl now*: From the children's book collection of A.G. Burwell.

His jaws were no doubt the strongest in the world. Joel managed to guzzle his entire bottle of milk without ever holding it. He needed his hands liberated to dismantle things. He simply wanted to understand how everything worked, a notion he also applied for things like walking and talking.

Tackling the steps, he spent due time sitting at the bottom of the staircase just staring at it. When he deemed himself ready, he crawled up the staircase as if he had been doing it forever. He took a similar approach with talking. At almost two years old, his pediatrician had referred us to a speech therapist. As if Joel knew, his grunts transformed into full sentences before we had the chance to make an appointment.

With few children residing in our neighborhood, Joel and Danielle had each other to play with. Despite their chronic ear infections, they were happy, easy going and always had something to do. Danielle devoted endless hours to reading or creating fractured fairytales on the computer. Sometimes it took a fly or a spider in the vicinity to break her concentration. She intensely despised them and refused to share any space in their company. Ordinarily, our dog rescued her by eating them. Joel had a sense of humor that was apparent even as a toddler. As with most toys that were not operated in the way that they were intended, Joel and his sister ran a remote control car down to the bottom of the staircase for a big crash. John sternly called out Danielle's name, who replied, "It's not me." No surprise. John rolled his eyes and called Joel's name in a matching tone. Joel, without hesitation passed the buck, "The dog did it." We tried to hide our laughter.

For all of their toys, a favorite pastime was sitting or playing together in a large cardboard box or the laundry basket. Danielle remained her brother's protector. Joel looked up to his big sister and mimicked her every move. Together, they played, they argued, they giggled and they always looked out for one another. For all their trivial worries or minor ailments, they both learned very young that a nice warm bath healed almost everything.

We followed John's family traditions making our own annual vacations sacred. Our best outings were at the beach amid the extended family. We rented an entire row of suites to be near one another. Ocean or pool, Cheryle was ordinarily found in the water surrounded with nieces and nephews, teaching them to be better swimmers. Evenings were filled with barbecues and games on the patio of the inn that overlooked the beach. Dining out was reserved for our last vacation day since service at the restaurants always took a long time with so many of us. I recall the proud feeling when Joel chose a photo of about twenty of us at one of those beach dinners for his second grade project to portray his family.

Living so close to the national capital offered us a wide range of affordable activities. The Smithsonian Museums, including the zoo, were free. Our former happy hours and John's sailing shifted to the soccer field for our children's games. John started a new hobby, woodworking. One of his first creations was a wooden swing set which included a handcrafted two-seater horse so the children could sit together.

Without family nearby, we relied heavily on one another for everything day to day. On class nights, I left after a hurried dinner together. The children adored their father who kept them well entertained. They made home videos, he read to them and put them to bed. My favorite video was that of John encouraging Joel to walk at eighteen months. Danielle, acutely aware of her brother's lack of interest, protectively jumped to his rescue. Wrapping her arms around him, she pulled him away from dad shouting, "Let him go. If he doesn't want to walk, he doesn't have to walk!" When my classes fell on weekends, John dropped me off at school then took the children to the Lincoln Memorial or to feed the ducks at the park nearby.

A challenge for our little family was John's work that required frequent travel. His project on a voice communication system for the air traffic system was in its final stages. As such, he was assigned to one of the teams providing oversight for its installation around the country. His mother, Helen, then retired, oftentimes planned her visits around John's travel to help with the children. She did not have other grandchildren so ours were the light of her life. My parents visited more frequently and their stays lengthened since Mom's work in the dress factory had significantly slowed. With labor moving overseas, one by one, the factories in our area were closing. During Mom's visits, we joked that our laundry basket had a hole in it because it stayed empty. In addition, she ironed everything in our closets whether it needed it or not. Jennifer and Jacelyn also spent time with us in the summers. Jacelyn taught Danielle, who was an early riser, to sleep in. She still awakened early then she snuggled in the day bed with Jacelyn where they snoozed for a few more hours. Our children loved the family visits and never went to daycare during those times.

On typical workdays, we dropped off the children at a daycare nearby. It also provided transportation to the elementary school that Danielle attended. Separation had always been a bit melodramatic for our daughter so we invented a goodbye ritual. At her previous daycare, we incorporated a kiss between each slat of the banister as we descended the stairs until our lips no longer reached. Nowadays, she and her brother, standing on his tiptoes, watched through the classroom window until we reached the parking lot. Before climbing into our car, we stopped to wave and throw one last air kiss.

One morning, I dropped them off a bit later, alone. My day of leave had been dedicated to cramming for mid-terms scheduled for that evening. Suffice it say that my clumsiness had not improved over the years, it took no more than a toothpick to lose my balance. As a matter of fact, my falls had become a family joke. On that particular morning, I simply slipped off the curb while waving to my children. Dropping out of their view, a confused Danielle told her teacher that she was unable to see me, perhaps I had "bent down to pick some flowers." He discretely moved the children away from the window then came to my aid. Unable to put weight on my right foot, Danielle's teacher drove me home. The odd heavy feeling in my right arm as I unlocked the front door should have been a clue. Ignoring the arm, I iced my ankle. Less than an hour later, excruciating pain in my arm forced me to call John from work to take me to the emergency room.

A few hours later, I hopped out of the hospital in an ankle brace and one crutch. My other arm was in a cast. There was no time left to devote to my mid-terms. Luckily, the painkillers made it bearable enough not to miss them. My technical classes had always generated more anxiety but that day, I felt oddly confident. Reality set in the following week when the professor returned the test, mumbling, "Don't take exams while you're on meds." I had barely passed. My saving grace was that practically the whole class had failed it, so he offered a retest and averaged the two grades. Exams for my literature classes were predominantly essays. That professor had offered me an oral exam. After a few preliminary questions, he entrusted me in an empty classroom to finish the exam on a cassette recorder.

Our family visit to Fountain Hill over the following weekend went as planned. Amid our typical prolonged Italian goodbyes, Mom had placed a small bag near our car. Confused, I asked where she was going. Quite as a matter of fact, she replied, "You are in a boot. Your arm is broken. You can't change the poor baby's diaper like that. You're going to hurt him." There was no rebuttal to that. Apparently, she had prearranged for the time off with her work. She simply squeezed in the backseat of our Subaru station wagon surrounded by the children and the dog and off we went. Pop picked her up two weeks later.

We saw our families often and continued to alternate our major holidays between John's and mine. My siblings were all settled with families of their own near Mom and Pop so it made more sense for us to travel for the holidays.

Elisa's dream job came to fruition. She worked in the design division of a swimsuit factory. The girls in our family never lacked swimsuits and always sported the most creative designs with Aunt Elisa's personal touch. The most unique was for our daughter who, as a baby, disliked sand on her body. Aunt

Elisa came to her rescue by creating a bright psychedelic swimsuit that essentially covered her entire body.

Alfredo worked full time in a technical manufacturing company while finishing his degree at LaSalle University. He later became a director at a pharmaceutical company. He and his wife, Cheryle, were very involved in their community. Alfredo was inducted in the Knights of Columbus and along with his wife, they became Eucharistic ministers and served in their church. Alfredo still loved to play basketball and coached Michael's team through his young years.

Gino married Kimberly. Soon after, he started his own construction business specializing in stucco. He later decided to manage a bar on the outskirts of town, a dream Pop had when we lived in *City Heurteau*. Gino had also inherited the storyteller gene. No matter how often we heard his same crazy stories, we laughed to the point of tears each and every time. He and Kimberly had three children: Andrew, Nicholas and Makenna. Gino, always a kid at heart, organized fun projects with his children. He taught them to fish, hunt and other outdoors activities. He still loved cars and racing. As a family, they spent many weekends together racing in a Micro Sprint 270 series[24] at the local racetrack. His passion led him to build a tiny track on his property for the children. As he got older, Gino swapped the three-wheeler of long ago for motorcycle rides under the blue sky. He became involved in various fundraisers through his volunteer work as the representative for a chapter in Pennsylvania's Bikers Against Bullies USA, a children's awareness program for anti-bullying campaigns in cooperation with the school system.

As for our parents, now that Pop was freed from his responsibilities to save us, he relaxed more. He and Mom even took vacations. They had embarked on numerous cruises to the Caribbean and South America with my siblings. Above all, they were magnificent role models and loved each of their grandchildren as much as they, in turn, loved their Nana and Popop.

Over time, our "francoameritalian" family gathered four generations and friends around Mom and Pop's dinner table. Newly formed couples continued to sync up calendars so we could all be together regularly. Having done away with the children table long ago, we simply joined tables together to accommodate everyone. We still cooked two full meals for Thanksgiving. One holiday in particular, the weight in the center of the table caused it to cave in. Fortunately, plenty of hands were available around the table to save the food.

Christmases at home were spectacular. They blended old and new traditions. The banister was lined with a stocking for each grandchild that was filled with socks, small trinkets and some candy. Our feast began on Christmas Eve with

---

[24] Micro Sprint: The smallest version of the "Sprint" car.

baccala. The linguini was now topped with more seafood and a marinara sauce. Christmas Day was a gluttony of pasta with a red meat sauce, chicken with roasted potatoes accompanied by a green salad.

Our antipasto meant stepping into a magical room in their cellar full of what later came to be called gourmet foods. Gleaming from their glass homes were Mom's canned lupine beans, marinated eggplant and olives. Over the years, our gatherings incorporated tastings from each of our homemade wines. Thankfully, we bought pre-pressed grape juice, so no stomping was necessary.

After our drawn-out gluttony, the women gathered to chat, the children played together and the men washed the dishes. A new tradition for our husbands, or perhaps a clever strategy to quickly clear space for their card games. Only four played at one time and they always stopped when friends dropped in throughout the day. More notably, the games were now smoke free.

Despite not smoking and his departure from the coal mine long ago, Pop's cough continued to worsen. When he was diagnosed with silicosis, it surprised us but not him. His labored breathing forced him to slow down considerably, granted he still worked hard by most standards. John joked about Pop only having two speeds, fast and stop.

When Pop turned fifty-five, the steel fabrication company closed its doors while the workers were on strike. It was not necessarily a bad thing for Pop. It allowed him to transfer to lighter work with the Allied company for another ten years until his retirement. He held a position in maintenance and was also responsible for all the logistics of setting up for conferences and some artistic events. His post was at Lehigh University where he was always well-liked by those he worked with, especially the cafeteria staff who consistently prepared foods that they knew he liked.

We unnecessarily worried about Pop being bored after his retirement. In reality, not much had changed. Between periods of persistent respiratory difficulties, he still helped all of us with projects, and loved spending time with the grandchildren. To preserve Pop's health, John hesitated to give him projects. One day, as we pulled into our driveway after work, Mom was playing with the children in the yard while Pop, wearing his sandals and white socks, was raking the mulch away from the slate pavers on the walkway between the gate and the front porch. Pop didn't like the feel of sweaty feet so regardless of his choice of shoes, he always wore socks. He never cared about how it was perceived. He also hated mulch. In his view, it looked messy. After tactfully voicing to Pop that John had intentionally placed the mulch there, Pop simply replied, "Ok. Today I take it off. Tomorrow I put it back." Clearly bored, he had made his point. John caved, at the same time, he cautiously spaced out the projects so Pop was not compelled to finish everything in one day.

117

In step with our children growing up, John enrolled Danielle in soccer at age five. Missing every practice and almost every game, reemphasized some challenges with going to college part time as a parent. As important as my studies had once been, my priorities had shifted. First and foremost, I refused to become a part-time mom. John understood, yet he persuaded me to stay in school.

As an alternative, I transferred to a university that offered a quarterly program instead of the traditional semester and temporarily reduced my work hours to half time. My classes were still in the evenings and some weekends, just longer class hours. More significantly, it allowed me to complete my program of studies more rapidly. My days off were spent with the children. Their bedtime was 7:30 so I did not miss too much. On non-school days, after dinner Danielle sat with me at the kitchen table doing homework. She had her very own spiral notebook that she carried everywhere to copy letters and words from her favorite books. Her dedication carried through school for the years to come.

There was not a single exam without notes in one hand and one of the children in my arms at the pediatricians' office due to their chronic ear infections, asthma and everything else that little people get. The asthma was discovered on one of the coldest nights of the year during a severe ice storm. A strange noise had awakened us around three in the morning. Annoyed, our immediate thoughts went to our dog chasing rabbits in her dreams again. Suddenly, we realized it was coming from the other side of our bedroom wall. That horrid sound was our two year old son's labored breathing. That night was his first ride to the hospital by ambulance. Joel was fascinated by the sirens. He was terribly disappointed that he did not get to ride the ambulance home the next day.

My self-imposed goal to graduate before Danielle started first grade was realized in spring of 1994. Delighted for simply being finished, participating in my graduation ceremony had never even been a consideration. Apparently, my family thought it differently. Mom, Pop and Elisa articulated that nothing would prevent them from missing the first person in our immediate family to graduate from college, never mind finishing summa cum laude. They left me with an even more difficult choice to make. Due to the large size of our class, we were limited to three tickets per graduate. Not wanting to disappoint anyone, I had additional tickets printed. Yes, those were desperate times! The extra tickets were a wise choice, John's mother decided that she was not missing this occasion either.

118

The ceremony took place at the Kennedy Center in Washington, D.C. My relatives knew that they had forged tickets. Warning them not to dilly dally, simply drop the ticket with the attendant then quickly enter into the hall, went on deaf ears. My sister dropped hers into the box. With the assistance of the attendant, she retrieved a real one to keep as a souvenir.

As our class entered through the large doors to the traditional Pomp and Circumstance, my eyes swept the grand hall for my loved ones. They were all proudly huddled together fiercely waving from the balcony. As our names were announced one by one, we climbed the few steps onto the stage to accept our diplomas. Solely focused on not tripping, I never heard my name. With the diploma firmly in my hand, feeling like a proud little girl with a strawberry *boule*, I blew air kisses their way prior to stepping off the stage. Standing there that day would have been impossible without their encouragement, inspiration and confidence in me. Ironically, on our drive home, Danielle exposed their wagers as to when I would trip getting across the stage.

My degree immediately opened doors for new career possibilities. A few months prior to graduation, a former colleague had offered me a position that nearly doubled my salary on a similar project that dealt with modernizing the aviation system. The only downside was that it ended my ideal arrangement of working part time.

Although I still found myself motivated by challenging work with opportunities for advancement, my priorities had changed over time and, interestingly, advancement took on a somewhat different meaning. Being a women and identifying myself as a parent first, posed some workplace challenges. Devoting myself exclusively to a company was not a goal since I did not want my family to become second to anything. However, in leadership or technical domains, men were still predominantly favored and perceived as more committed to the company. Divulging my true frame of mind could have been disastrous for my career. To balance work and family, I arrived at work very early in the mornings and often took work home to resume after the children went to sleep. My managers provided me with a lot of flexibility to telework before teleworking was even a thing which was a huge aid since our children were sick a lot. Being a firm believer that having it all did not exist, I consistently juggled my choices depending on what was most important at the time without jeopardizing the rest. Sometimes it was work and sometimes it was family.

With John and I both working full time, it allowed us to settle in our forever home during the spring of 1994. Moving less than three miles left us in the same excellent school district, along with a commute to work that remained relatively unchanged. The 1950 contemporary style of the home added to its character. The huge yard was half wooded, the rest served as an enormous playground for our children and the dog. Although the home was structurally sound, its outdated flair became one huge project for John who had evolved into quite the handyman and, in my opinion, had missed his calling in carpentry.

Our new neighborhood was well established with families who had settled in around the early 1950s when their homes were constructed. It was a lovely rarity for such a transient area to be welcomed with homemade strawberry pies and honey. The neighborhood held a picnic each fall. That day, the road was closed to traffic for the neighbors to safely gather, the grills were fired up and the children took over the street. In that warm atmosphere was our virtual front porch of Fountain Hill with a sprinkle of life from our *Rue Taffin*.

Danielle and Joel played together in the yard, in cardboard boxes and their new thing was to build what Joel, now almost five, coined as an Italian room in his bedroom. It was essentially a fort made with sheets and blankets. More often than not, he too wore sandals with socks because he found it more comfortable. The first time noticing it, I casually mentioned that we don't normally wear socks with sandals. With a confused look, he retorted that, "Popop wears them this way all the time." He was absolutely right! He called me on violating my own basic principle about being "yourself."

It was also the age of little people's birthday parties. Lots of them. Joel, oddly declared that he did not want a birthday party. It was mind-blowing that a sociable five year old, who was typically direct and articulate, had made that choice for no apparent reason. He and Danielle both loved apple pie, so I promised to bake one. It was still, "No thank you." Question after question, we were left clueless. One morning, when I reminded him of an early pick up from pre-school for a doctor's appointment, the color drained from his face. He quickly retorted with, "But I told you I don't want a birthday party." There it was! Apparently, he had remembered that on his last annual physical, the pediatrician reassured Joel that he would not need to worry about shots until his fifth birthday. Eliminating the party, eliminated his birthday and the shot! Needless to say, Joel was not only vaccinated, he had a great time at his birthday party.

The children played sports throughout elementary school: soccer during spring and fall, basketball and indoor soccer in the winter. At that age, Danielle was athletic with a greater focus in the social dimension of the game. She was more likely to be caught running down the field hand-in-hand with a friend as the coach screamed game instructions around them. Joel, also athletic, was attentive to the tactics of winning the game. For those things of particular interest, he spent endless hours practicing at home to perfect his skills. For his fifth birthday, we surprised him with a basketball and a hoop since he had recently joined a team and was preparing for his very first game. He was so thrilled that he took his basketball to bed that night.

Around five o'clock in the morning, we jumped out of bed startled by the doorbell. We were stunned to find Joel on the other side of the door still wearing the boxers and a long t-shirt that he had slept in. Tucked around one arm, was his new basketball. At some point during the night, he felt compelled to practice hoops in the driveway, then accidentally locked himself out. We were more disturbed that he had managed to get outside of the house without being heard.

The small elementary school that our children attended was nearby. Danielle loved her school and was an excellent student. While she was on the shy side, she was always engaged in various extracurricular activities. As a patrol for two years, she accompanied young students with special needs to and from their buses. Always very thoughtful, she had a keen sense to seek out those who felt alone.

By the fifth grade, students were offered an opportunity to learn how to play an instrument. Danielle chose the saxophone. The instrument had grown in popularity since the president of the United States, Bill Clinton, played it. When the number of saxophonists exploded, the music teacher formed two groups to repeat the score at the concert. Totally disinterested in working an entire school year only to play a half concert, Danielle opted for a less popular instrument, the oboe.

In 1996, Joel began his kindergarten. Eager to follow in his big sister's footsteps, he organized his backpack during the afternoon before the first day of school. When my foot barely nudged it from the center of the room, I teasingly asked if he had filled it with rocks. His eyes confirmed it. They always did! He loved rocks and had collected quite a few over the years. Most were stashed in boxes under his bed. From his days at daycare, regardless of how much fun he was having, he immediately raced into our arms wrapping his legs around us, ready to go home. He always felt heavier at the end of the day since his pockets were jam-packed with rocks, sometimes weighing his pants down to his hips. It was logical that he had carefully bundled these treasures in a brown paper bag, duct-taped them for protection, and stuffed the rocks inside his backpack.

Joel and his best friend from daycare, Zak, both attended the same schools all the way through college. They had played on the same soccer and basketball teams through their middle school years. Their soccer skills had allowed them to play on elite competitive teams and win various championships. They both also loved the outdoors spending countless hours playing in the creek that flowed alongside Zak's house.

Joel's generosity and perceptiveness did not change much growing up. One of my most notable recollections was a children's Easter egg hunt at our church. A little girl was crying on the landing for some unknown reason. In mid-conversation and mid-stride, our six year old grabbed a handful of candy out of his basket and dropped it into her empty basket. No words were exchanged to us or the little girl that he did not know. She threw them back at him but he simply kept on walking.

In another incident some months later, he encouraged us to take part in an international children's sponsorship program. Barely able to write, he watched a specific channel waiting for its commercial to appear over and over, until he was able to write down the entire phone number on the back of a napkin. He climbed the stairs with the napkin in hand and voiced that, "There are many children who need food and clothes. We always have leftovers so that means we have enough to send money each month for those who don't have enough." Touched, we sponsored two children of the same ages as ours for all the years that followed.

With two children playing sports, our weekends were spent going from one game to another, almost always in opposite directions. When the games overlapped, John and I split the games then alternated for the next one. John also became a leader for Joel's den in Cub Scouts. Since most activities included the same group of children, we also formed lasting friendships with their parents.

Likewise, the more packed days meant speedy meals. In keeping with our tradition of eating together that, for me, had begun in France, busier days meant we all ate together a little later. Our go-to meal coined "pasta surprise" was easily prepared in twenty minutes or less. Essentially any assortment of vegetables found the fridge that we sautéed and mixed with a pasta. Pasta with peas quickly rose to first place. Since some habits were hard to break, leftovers were deliberate, just in case unexpected guests or friends of our children were at the house. Dinnertime had always been one of the most important parts of the day. We shared our daily happenings, although we frequently learned more by listening to our children's interaction with each other.

While there was no shortage of topics at dinnertime, gaps were easily filled with stories about my birthplace or my youth, a slice of a different world that I sought to keep alive. It was not entirely foreign to them since they had met aunts, uncles and cousins who had visited us from Italy over the years. Totally unexpected, one day over supper, John proposed a family trip to Italy for our children to make better connections to the stories of yesteryear.

In that vein, during the summer of 2000, we combined three weeks of tours and family stopovers in Italy and Switzerland. We made a loop to visit the entire family, some of whom were known to me only in stories, some I had not seen in a half of a century and others that I knew we would never see again. One fabulous week was spent in Switzerland with Cousin Paolo and his wife. His father, Franco was now deceased but we met other cousins and Paolo's mother for the first time.

By train, we rolled along massive fields of rice and spectacular sunflowers on our way to visit Mom's two older sisters, Felice and Filomena, in Turin. In transit, John asked if I knew Zia Felice who was meeting us at the train station. I confessed to knowing her only through stories shared by my parents. Exiting the train, his worries dissolved immediately. In the distance, even John could not mistake the face flooded with tears that belonged to the hands that were wildly waving, for someone else. Zia was an older version of my mother.

An overnight train took us to my native village of *Orsara*. We stayed with the Simonelli family. My godparents were deceased but we remained close with their four children. Their home adjoined the tabacchi store where our children loved to "help." Our week in *Orsara* was spent amid family with countless walks throughout the village where every corner had a connection to my stories. The authentic décor of the fountain where Mom had spent hours doing laundry was what truly manifested the imprint of the past. I pointed out the place where their grandmother invariably arrived very early in the morning to take the first place at the trough. Water flowed down so you needed to be upstream, at the top of the line, for clean water. Joel observed the hard stone where she knelt and asked if she did laundry in the winter too. "Yes," I said, "But first, she had to chip off the ice that formed on top of the water." Our nine year old son thought for a moment, then said, "This is really beautiful Mom, but I am sorry that you all had to live like this."

Almost everyone in town knew my parents. Our neighbors still remembered our "happy house" of long ago. Wherever we went, I was recognized as either Michelino Russo's daughter or Leonarda Russo's granddaughter. When we knocked on the door of the house where I was born, the proprietors invited us in for a chat about their old friends in America, a tour and an espresso.

Before we had left for that adventure, we asked Pop if there was anyone specific that he wished for us to visit on his behalf. He gave me one name that was unfamiliar to me followed by "the look" when seeking an address. He recommended that we walk toward the Piazza, then stop and ask anyone, everyone knew where one and all lived. Accordingly, a gentlemen pointed us to the right door where I was promptly recognized as my father's daughter before introducing myself. We talked for hours over espresso and a small feast of pastries, prosciutto and cheeses. What Pop had failed to mention, was that the couple once worked as village midwives and had brought me, my sister and my deceased brother into the world.

Our adventure ended with a week discovering Rome, Florence and Sienna. In that experience of a lifetime, our children had made new friends, extended their family circle and discovered a vital part of their history.

The following summer, our cousin's daughter, Anna, from *Orsara*, spent several months with us. Her desire to perfect her English aligned with our need to have someone stay with the children for part of the summer. That visit amplified extended family get-togethers that allowed Anna to meet the rest of her family.

We squeezed in some sightseeing, the Smithsonian Museums and a short excursion to the beach. The beach weather was not ideal but tolerable, plus the water was choppier than normal. People being permitted in the water had made the danger less apparent. By mid-afternoon, our escapade spiraled into a catastrophe. Joel had made a new best friend. The pair played together in the ocean while the rest of us sat on a blanket chitchatting with our eyes on the little ones. Through the crowds on the beach, my only recollection was meeting the fear in Joel's eyes in the distance. Never feeling the sand under my feet, I flew to a few feet away from him. The father of his new friend had already jumped in. With one sweep, he snatched Joel from the riptide and threw him into my arms. The man remained prisoner of the current and was, in turn, rescued by the lifeguard. The two boys played cards on the blanket for the rest of the afternoon.

By morning, the beach was closed. Search and rescue teams in the air and in the water combed the ocean for a father and son who had not been as fortunate. Months later, we learned from Joel's teacher that she was troubled by a story that he had written in his daily journal about that event. Joel did not talk about it, but in his journal, he voiced that he had lived because it was not his time to leave this world. She wanted to know if the story was true.

With the rhythm of seasons, our children grew older. Danielle entered middle school, which in our area was sixth through eighth grade. It was her benchmark to convince us that she was sufficiently mature to abandon her afterschool daycare. Recalling my youth of disagreeing with our own parents' position on various things, the words rang in my head, "When I become a parent, I will do things differently." Well, when it was all said and done, we were more liberal than my parents but we were strict nonetheless. Likewise, my perspective had changed on some of my most detested rules as a child because when the responsibility fell on me, they did not appear so stringent. Intensely echoing in my head were also the words from a grieving friend of some years prior who had lost his grandson in a tragic car accident...*Nothing can change what has happened to us. Your second child will arrive soon.*

Remember that you are the parent and you are responsible for your children. Make every decision knowing that you will need to live with your choices.

In tandem with the afterschool house rules imposed, our dog pitched in. Her friendliness was well concealed by the sound of her bark when anyone, other than family, was nearing our door. Upon arriving home, our expectations were to relock the doors behind them and to promptly telephone one of us. Friends were not permitted in the house until we returned from work. That was the price for independence!

Joel was three years behind his sister, however we were a bit more hesitant with him. He was our rule bender and forgot things. On his first day of independence, even after repeated reminders, Joel not only failed to make the call, he never answered ours. Nearly an hour after his expected arrival home, I left work. As my car made its turn onto our street, Joel and a friend were energetically practicing hoops in our driveway. Upon seeing my face, Joel's memory was mysteriously restored. His face paled in understanding the gravity of the situation. He simply stated that he had forgotten!

One of our community's finest assets was the cultural richness brought forth by the diversity characteristic to our area. One school in particular was well-known for having a student population from approximately eighty different nationalities with over forty different languages spoken. Another marvelous feature was their music enrichment program. Danielle rapidly shifted from sports to music. Joel focused on soccer and music during his middle school years. Eventually his concentration tilted more toward music. He played oboe too. Both children shined in music, receiving various distinctions and awards for their oboe solos and choral accompaniments in competitions. Danielle's first solo and ensemble piece was "Pachelbel's Canon." A few years later, she heard Joel play it for one of his competitions. As he walked out of the room, she explicitly told him that he would play it for her wedding, someday. Their transition from middle to high school was reasonably stress-free. That was owed primarily to the cohesive partnership of the music directors around our community public schools.

In high school they both quickly found their home in music. In symphonic band they played the oboe. In marching band, they played the Marimba, timpani, bongos and various other stationary instruments with the percussion ensemble. Band meant summer camp. As a freshman, band and camp made for a less traumatic first day of school as they already knew about one hundred students across the grade levels. Their band family spent a great deal of time together and formed strong bonds. As Danielle and Joel became more passionate about their music, we easily transitioned from soccer parents to band parents. John volunteered on the pit crew to transport and set up the stationary

125

instruments for competitions at their various venues. My time was devoted to fund raisers and chaperoning. Between us, we participated in almost all of the musical, academic and sports events.

Danielle was very driven, passionate and always put a lot of pressure on herself. For her first high school all-District symphonic ensemble audition, we spent our entire drive home with a distraught daughter reliving the imperfections of her presentation. To calm her, we promised to drive her back after all the auditions were over to view the results that would be posted on the front doors of the school. To distract her, on their return trip a few hours later, John took a small detour and bought her the pea coat, a youth sport coat that she had wanted for some time. When they arrived at the school, some of the upper classman already there rushed to congratulate her. It was an honor to qualify for this event at any grade level and particularly difficult as a freshman.

Throughout high school, the children both placed in district and state competitions and received numerous distinctions for their solo performances. At their respective graduations, both were presented with the Semper Fidelis Award for musical excellence by the United States Marines Youth Foundation.

At that age of being a bit perturbed, our sweet and kind little girl emerged here and there. The shoot of lily of the valley offering on May Day to remind me of the fragrant ride in the woods in *City Heurteau* propagated for the many years yet to come. Now and again, she wrote a note or a poem, just because. What also had not changed was her fear of flies and spiders. Her bedroom door stayed closed to keep them out which was a definite plus since her mounds of clothes and books covering the bed and floor were also out of my view. Maggie, our dog, no longer came to her rescue. A bee sting inside her mouth ended her bug eating days. Desperate, Danielle sometimes offered her brother a dollar to clear her room of insects. Although he would have done it for free, he was always happy to pocket his sister's money.

Somewhere below insects was riding the school bus after school. Danielle conveniently missed it every day, "forcing" her to ride home with friends. She was driven to school in the mornings. It put me at work a bit later, but I treasured my time with her since the evenings were typically filled with homework and activities. It was a relatively short and pretty muted journey to school until the radio played Lee Ann Womack's "I Hope You Dance." We glanced at one another in a complicit smile. It was my song for her. Our favorite time of the year was between Thanksgiving and Christmas when one of the radio stations only played Christmas songs. Despite our wordless rides, they always ended with Danielle leaning in for a kiss. Frequently, the only words ever exchanged were "love you" and "love you too." Luckily, it was a short walk to drop off her oboe in the band room. Being the queen of flip-flops she

126

owned a pair in every color and wore them year round. In the event of rain or snow, she decorated her feet in toe socks.

As chaperones, John or I often drove our minivan to assist with field trips, music or sporting activities. When Danielle joined the squad for winter color guard, I drove a group of girls to their competitions on Saturdays. Their eight minute routine was an all-day affair. In all of their activities, what we cherished most were the opportunities to get to know the friends who were part of our children's lives. One in particular was one of Danielle's closest friends, Mary. She had a warm smile and was exceptionally kind. More often than not, they spent their weekends together at our house rehearsing their instruments or working on various school projects. The inseparable girls mostly behaved like five-year-olds: jumped on beds, decorated T-shirts for any occasion and laughed a lot.

High school life was simplified for a year when Joel entered as a freshmen. Transportation to school and activities was less complicated since Danielle was a senior and had obtained her driver's license. Their common music interest and commitments allowed them to spend time together among friends. Amid concerts and musical competitions, our weekends remained family events.

The apple did not fall too far from the tree. Although our children visited friends, we always encouraged them to invite friends over. Extra food was prepared for dinner, just in case someone stayed. On day, while chitchatting with a friend at the grocery store, she applauded me for preparing pasta for a large group of students prior to the high school homecoming dance. My blank stare was reciprocated by a chuckle followed by, "I guess you haven't read the *A-Blast*." On my way home, I picked up a copy of the school newspaper and read all about the progressive dinner that my children and their friends had planned in lieu of going to a restaurant. Pasta would be served at our house. Three days later, we hosted seventeen friends!

Intertwined with the good, there were also some difficulties, mostly around health issues in the family that were becoming more problematic. Elisa, suffered a heart attack at fifty seven. She healed but as usual, resumed her normal life more quickly than she should have. John's mother was exhibiting signs of dementia. Since she lived far and alone, it was impossible to monitor. Meanwhile Pop's health deteriorated by the day. His breathing had become much more labored and his trips to the hospital were more frequent. He had already been on oxygen for a few years. He was no longer chatty. More often than not, he gave a hurried "hello" on the phone and passed the handset to Mom.

Complicating matters, an aortic aneurism that was discovered completely by accident, obligated Pop to undergo open heart surgery. That procedure took a huge toll on his already weakened system. Getting from one room to another became even more labored. Nevertheless, each and every day, he dressed, shaved and read the newspaper. Never keen on being confined, he extended the hose for his oxygen throughout the entire house, including the front porch and the back yard. His outings, however, became more taxing and eventually impossible. The summer of 2006 was Pop's last visit in Virginia to celebrate Danielle's high school graduation.

Danielle began college that fall. Our conversations with our children in regards to college were mostly around their choice of a large, medium or small school. Danielle had fallen in love with Florence so her criteria included a study abroad program in Italy. She had alerted us that her French studies would be replaced with Italian in college to meet that goal. She and her dear friend Mary both wanted to become elementary school teachers. Still joined at the hip, they were beyond thrilled when they were both accepted at their choice school, Virginia Tech. The girls embarked on this journey which was about four hours south, with Mary's dad, Peter.

We followed the next day with a carload of furnishings for Danielle's dorm. After spending a few days on campus to help organize her dorm, purchase textbooks and get the lay of the campus, it was time to separate. After breakfast, John failed miserably to rush our goodbyes on a blazing hot morning. Driving away from campus, my eyes lingered on them through the passenger side mirror. The girls were huddled together on the side of the road, beaming with happiness. Smiling, I voiced to John, "They are going to be OK. They are so happy. This is their future and they will be great together."

That same year, Joel started his sophomore year in high school. Prior to getting his driver's license, we had a similar arrangement in the mornings, except Joel was much chattier than his sister during our drive to school. Our precious sunrise chats covered everything and nothing. By then, he had become fully immersed in music. He was part of several school chorus groups and he too excelled at the oboe, taking first chair in symphonic band. In the fall, he played stationary percussion instruments in the marching band. Joel was always full of surprises. Chatting with Zak's mom, she had remarked about how much she enjoyed hearing Joel play the piano. Ginny had known Joel since pre-school when the boys played in their stream. Perhaps she was thinking of someone else. She enlightened me, apparently he tuned it and played when visiting their home.

Another revelation, for as much as we had hoped, Joel had not outgrown his asthma. For a long time, he and Pop took identical medications. On Joel's more problematic days, John or I teleworked. His attacks often required urgent medical visits. On one trip to the doctor, which was only minutes from our house, for an unrelated issue, he had an attack on the way there. Upon our arrival, they called for an ambulance. Joel was Joel. Exiting their parking lot, he yanked the oxygen mask from his face and gestured that the sirens were not on. Chuckling, the paramedic promised to give him the works. Over the years, we had gotten to know the clinicians at all of his schools. High school posed the biggest challenge since his studies were more demanding. He missed weeks at a time but, interestingly, he always found a way to keep up with all of his musical commitments.

By the end of summer 2006, Pop, almost seventy two, was at his worst. He spent more time in the hospital than out. Extended confinement to a bed caused his legs to weaken significantly and necessitated rebuilding his strength at a rehabilitation center. Pop was devastated and worse, rehab did not help. Meanwhile, his health in general continued to decline forcing a return trip to the hospital.

A distance that had never separated us suddenly became a challenge. My siblings kept me informed, but it was not the same as being there. I so wished to be closer for Pop's more difficult times. Days after his last hospital admission, the doctor suggested a family meeting which I attended remotely. We all knew that he was very ill, nevertheless, we were not prepared for what we heard. His doctor delicately explained the state of Pop's prognosis. He had but six months. In honor of his wish to return home, a hospital bed took the center of his dining room and palliative care was set up. I arrived the day he was discharged from the hospital. With my siblings, we explored additional routine day-to-day care to assist our parents.

Pop was Pop. He made his own plans. Three days after his release from hospital, my brother and I held his hand as he drifted into his future in the afterworld. He had fulfilled his dream for us, one that had never wavered since it began so long ago while serving in the cavalry of Piedmont. It was that dream, one that came with difficult and painful choices that led our family to a place of hope for a bright future. A dream that had never been about having it all, but simply about having all that was important. He left in peace, surrounded by the family that he adored and who adored him.

The year that followed was colored by love, grief, and sorrow. Family life without Pop was hard for all of us. Alfredo principally took care of Mom's day to day needs: paying bills, grocery shopping and running to her house at all hours to fix this or that. Even the remote control for the TV became an emergency, mostly due to user error or, sometimes, it simply needed new batteries. She was lonely, and she deeply missed Pop who had always taken care of everything. Her driver's license was useless since she had not driven in years, something we had all agreed should remain that way. To simplify life, she sold "our home" and moved in with Alfredo and Cheryle.

Meanwhile, their careers were progressing. Work advancements involved a major move for Alfredo and Cheryle out of the area. For Mom, accompanying them was probably the best choice, nevertheless, it was one that no one was prepared for. It hit everyone hard. After a bit of fuss, it was Gino, "the baby" who reminded us of our pact some thirty years earlier that was still engrained in his memory. It brought everyone back to reason. Accordingly, we promised one another that no matter how far apart we lived, we will always do our best to be together for the holidays. A promise we kept to each other and Mom for the many years to come.

Living with Alfredo and Cheryle, the love of Pop's life and queen of the dance floor at the Dancing Café of *City Heurteau* spent her time knitting "coming home from the hospital outfits" for each of the grandchildren's new arrivals. On nicer days, she developed a love-hate relationship with the geese at the pond at the edge of their property.

John's mother was also aging. John did not want to force her into doing anything that she did not want to do. When the dementia significantly progressed, the time had arrived for a difficult decision as living alone became a hazard. We respectfully presented her with two options: living with us or moving into an assisted living center. We removed her biggest worry by offering to take Barney, her sevenish year old dog. She opted for the assisted living center but wished to be near to us. A few weeks later, we moved Helen a few miles from our home where even Barney was invited to visit her regularly. Barney adapted well to our home and lived a very long life…he was eighteen, so almost a million when he crossed the rainbow bridge.

With the arrival of spring 2007, life began to have a sense of normal again. On Easter weekend, Elisa and Dominic visited. Danielle came home from college. We were also celebrating Joel's sixteenth birthday. As usual, Mary, Zak and other school friends dropped in and out of our house watching movies, playing foosball and table tennis in our basement. It was those moments that we were glad our basement was cluttered with games that kept them at home. We laughed about there being no birthday at our home without the must-have apple pie. We feasted on Saturday so everyone could get on the road reasonably early on Sunday for their long journeys home. Mary, as usual, spent the night. The girls had planned to drive back to the university together on Sunday.

Normal ended a week later on April 16th. Joel woke up sick. Also exhausted from a very restless night, I chose to telework. A bad dream had left me unnerved and unable to focus. My only recollection of the dream was being at my children's funeral. It was beyond disturbing that these thoughts even existed in my head. It was even more difficult to escape them or admit to having them. That day only worsened to become the nightmare of all nightmares.

Elisa phoned asking if we had heard from Danielle. We had not. After that, the only words heard were "shooting" and "Virginia Tech." Hoping for a mistake, I grabbed the remote but every news channel confirmed it. In my other hand was my mobile that was desperately dialing and redialing Danielle, who I knew was in class. A few minutes later, John called to say he received a text from her saying that she was fine, but she was unable to reach Mary. Finally, one of my calls made it through and gave me comfort in hearing our daughter's voice. She told me that Mary had been in French class in the next building over and had not yet arrived for their subsequent class together. Cell service was sparse and her battery was low. The entire school was in lockdown. Mary's number was in my mobile so I told Danielle I would also call.

My numerous calls went directly to Mary's voicemail. In desperation, I phoned her father, Peter. He had not connected with his daughter yet. Cell phone service was saturated as everyone was calling their loved ones. I asked Joel to set me up with Instant Messaging which appeared to be the quickest way to connect with students who had eventually been released from their classrooms. Feeling completely useless at home, I decided to go to the university. Apparently, John had already left work with the same idea. Ginny collected Joel and we picked up Peter who still had not heard his daughter's voice.

John was always more reserved. In all of our years together, I had seen him cry twice. The first time was when we almost lost Jacelyn in a horrific car accident. The second was upon his return from work when I conveyed to him that we still had not heard from Mary. The long drive to the university felt even longer. It was late evening with still no news from Mary.

Twenty minutes before we arrived, Peter was simply broken after receiving a call from home. John's face went white as I noticed he placed his hand on Peter's. From the back seat, I wrapped my arms around Peter. John attempted to pull the car over to give Peter a bit of air and to tell me what I had not yet grasped, but he urged John to keep driving. Perhaps it was denial. All I knew was that I no longer had the ability to speak to my own daughter or anyone. I sent my last text to Danielle saying we would arrive at the inn shortly then my mobile was silenced, my eyes closed and we all rode the rest of the way in profound silence.

While John parked the car, we entered the inn, the place where no one wanted to be. It had been set up as the emergency center for family and friends to get information on their loved ones. I entered with Peter for support, but upon hearing the words that our sweet Mary was one of the victims, the raw pain rendered me completely useless. The rest of the evening was a blur. It paled against any challenge we had ever faced. There was no place to hide, despair and pain was heard and felt everywhere.

In that dreadful reality, I found John, a ghost against a wall with countless other ghosts all lined up who were either waiting to hear about their loved ones or attempting to remove themselves from the horrifying cries coming from every corner of the inn. The walls suddenly disappeared, and that darkness that I had feared forever found me. Completely surrendering my mind and heart to it, the darkness held me suspended in time with no base or walls to cling to.

Suddenly, among a mass of wounded sounds between me and the entryway, a single hollow and distorted voice called "Mom!" I knew it belonged to my daughter. When our eyes met, I tried to speak and although the words didn't come, she knew. My heart shattered as I held her and watched my baby girl's heart crumble before mine. When I looked up, John was there holding her too. No one wanted to let go. A few minutes later, when we found Peter again, all we could do was watch him and Danielle hold one another in the deepest pain imaginable.

The avoided call to Joel was beyond hard. I did not want to call him until there was information, then I did not want to tell him the news. Saying those dreaded words made the nightmare real. After a very long silence, he only asked if she suffered. I could only say, "I hope not." My heart longed to hold him. It was a very long night for him too. We were very grateful that Zak's mom, Ginny, was there to comfort him. Much to my horror, my disturbing nightmare had come true. That day, a part of my children had died.

On that horrific day, thirty two lives with dreams and hopes were lost forever. They were teachers and children, "our children" who had done nothing wrong and were exactly where they were supposed to be. It was a very dark time, the difficult moments were countless. One that was particularly heartbreaking for me was going through some of Mary's personal belongings. When Danielle saw her soulmate's favorite grey sweat pants, she buried her face into it and cried, "Oh Mary I love you." Her shoulders gave away her silent tears as Mary's scent filled her heart. All I knew to do was say, "I love you and I will always be here for you when your heart hurts." We were all distraught and completely unprepared in guiding our children.

Our entire community mourned the tragedy. Danielle's network of remarkable friends formed a strong pillar of unwavering comfort for one another. They were all suffering and helped one another to heal. The shock was brutal but their solidarity was exemplary.

We had offered her the option to transfer to a different university. After some thoughtful reflection, she opted to stay at Virginia Tech. A choice that was not easy for her or us. She asserted that who else would understand what she was going through better than those who were going through the same thing. There was no normal path forward for two girls once joined through smiles, laughter and tears. It was difficult to even think of one without thinking of the other. Our daughter had always been strong but no one should need to be that strong. Gradually, we found our way to begin healing. Closure, on the other hand, for something so senseless was near impossible.

In the fall of the following school year, we hosted Ferdie as part of the high school Choral German Exchange Program. He and Joel instantly became two peas in a pod. Ferdie was a charismatic, bright young man who was particularly fascinated by our election system. On Election Day, he skipped his other activities to accompany me to the polling station. It turned out even better than anticipated. He was permitted to stand beside me as I cast my vote for Obama.

Since the exchange students were in the USA at the end of October, they had the opportunity to experience an American Halloween. Raiding an old box in our basement, Ferdie found some psychedelic bell bottoms, Elvis side burns and dark glasses. Joel simply grabbed a pair of my shorts that fit him like booty shorts along with a tank top that should have been discarded several sizes ago. After the party, a group of parents accompanied them to Joel's car. Between being a little distracted, being a new driver and not being accustomed to having to remember where the car was parked, he declared it stolen when he did not find it where he thought he had left it. Although it was one of the coldest days of the year, neither of the boys thought they needed coats. They searched the area in their eccentric and provocative outfits. Before the police arrived, they discovered the car a few blocks away, exactly where Joel had left it.

In the summer of 2008, Joel was selected by the high school to take part in a four-week program through the Governor School Visual and Performing Arts[25] held at the University of Richmond. The program promoted cultural and artistic enrichment classes for gifted children. In that setting, Joel was also expected to take academic classes. He loved everything about his curriculum, college life and new friends who had come from many different parts of the

---

[25] Governor School Visual and Performing Arts: Established in 1973 in Virginia by Lynwood Holton for gifted students in the discipline of academics and visual arts. It was an opportunity to offer possibilities to students beyond the typical programs offered at their base schools.

state. That opportunity became a significant turning point for Joel, evolving into a fabulous final year in high school.

Joel was always surrounded by friends. They even accompanied him on visits to Grandma at the assisted living center nearby. Sometimes she recognized him, sometimes not, but that did not deter him. Between his friends, band and choral commitments, Joel stayed busy and had tons of fun. On prom night, he missed his agreed upon curfew. When I finally broke down and dialed his cell, he responded my call with, "Hey Mom, you'll never believe it. I was crowned Prom King." We thought he was joking so he would not have to address the issue at hand. But no, he came home wearing the evidence.

Joel was always full of stories. He was high spirited and slightly impulsive with a big heart. We tended to worry a little bit more about him because he was also more adventurous. Although he had a tendency to make my hair stick straight up, always taking things close to the edge, he was growing up to be a wonderful human being. He had a fabulous finish to high school. His music achievement earned him various awards and distinctions. He was the first student in his school to earn a spot in All-State Band, All-State Chorus and Honor Chorus, all in the same year. In the summer, he was reunited with Ferdie in Germany as part of the choral exchange program. There they performed at various venues in Germany and Austria.

In fall 2009, Joel effortlessly adapted to college life VCU[26] where he pursued music performance for oboe. Joel and Danielle both had taken private lessons for years with a phenomenal oboist who played in the President's Own United States Marine Band. After he completed his military service, he was hired to teach at the VCU School of Performing Arts. At that point, there was no a question about Joel's college plans.

Bittersweet for us, after three semesters, Joel switched his major from music to Economics. He was cognizant that he enjoyed playing and doing gigs for pleasure, not necessarily for a living. Likewise, it freed his time to pursue other interests. In the winter, he played indoor soccer. His love for the outdoors attracted him to cycling. He joined the college cycling team who raced neighboring universities. He also worked part time at the university as a bicycle technician involved in an educational outreach program teaching students about cycling fitness and how to make their own bike repairs.

With both children in college at the same time for a few years, we were empty nesters. Life for our daughter remained a bit of an emotional rollercoaster. She always stayed busy and did very well in her studies. She worked a few hours a week at a children's learning center. She also adopted

---

[26] VCU: Virginia Commonwealth University; State University in Richmond, Virginia.

Eko, a furry companion. My worries about the additional responsibilities for the adorable black Boxador were unwarranted. Our daughter was remarkably responsible and after witnessing the love and comfort that her loyal friend brought her, it was a perfect union.

Danielle achieved her goal to study abroad. We talked on the phone almost every day while she was in Florence. A ritual that originated when she earned her freedom from her afterschool daycare of long ago now included me in her adventure. The evenings were reserved for Skyping with her boyfriend, Ryan, whom she had known since her early days at the university. Ryan was kind, smart and, most importantly, he adored our daughter. During Danielle's stay in Italy, Ryan, who studied aeronautical engineering, was involved in a summer internship in Washington, D.C. with the Federal Aviation Administration to analyze flight traffic information. During this period, he and the furry animals stayed with us. They both loved dogs and had two between them.

John and I met Danielle in Florence at the end of her program. She proudly guided us to all of her favorite places in the city that had enriched her life. We also spent a few days in Rome, Sienna and obviously a week in *Orsara*. There, the Simonelli family hosted us. Mario, now the elected Mayor of the village, took time off of his busy schedule to escort us on historical tours of *Orsara* and other sites around the region.

By her senior year at the university, Danielle had acquired all of her necessary credits which allowed her to take graduate level courses early. She and Ryan stayed at Virginia Tech for another year to complete their Master's diploma. That year, they were also engaged! Although Ryan had already revealed his secret to us a few months earlier, John was heartened when Ryan officially asked him for his daughter's hand in marriage.

After their graduate studies, we were overjoyed that they both found work in our area in their respective professional disciplines. Danielle taught in an elementary school and Ryan was employed as an aeronautical engineer. In their spare time, they ran marathons.

In June 2012, they married despite an unexpected Derecho storm that paralyzed most of the east coast. Power was out almost everywhere, including at our home, the venue for the wedding and the hotel hosting many of our guests. We were all freaked out. John's first reaction was to pull the bed sheet over his head hoping to ignore the situation. It was futile. Catastrophes and cell phone service never mixed well. When Danielle and I finally connected, we spoke quickly regarding the venue situation for fear of losing reception. The patrons wanted to move the date for a day when power was restored. She calmly stated the obvious, "Family and friends are all here. All we need is the officiant. The flowers, cake and electricity do not matter. We are getting married today."

A wedding that had taken a year to plan was re-planned in a few hours. Our air-conditioned hall was abandoned for an outdoor ceremony and reception under the natural light. Remarkably, everything was delivered on time. The staff used table linens to fan the icing that was melting on the cupcakes. The semi-wilted flowers were beautifully arranged on a table under a tree to protect them from the hot sun. As promised years prior, Joel played "Pachelbel's Canon" on oboe for his sister and his new brother. Even a pair of deer approached for a peek at the lovebirds who were both beaming with happiness as they exchanged their vows.

The tables, charmingly arranged on the patio, were adorned with a simple bouquet of fresh corals and greens on white tablecloths. The meal was superb. It was all prepared on charcoal grills that the country club had rented since the storm rendered their kitchen useless. Candles lined a path to the restrooms. The DJ brought his own generator. After dinner, the headlights on his car provided lighting for the dance floor. That incredible wedding day was ensued by a long honeymoon in Italy.

Joel returned to the university in the fall. He continued on his path, evolving into a very thoughtful and insightful adult. Of mention around that time was a particularly moving phone call from a very emotional Joel after he had left his class. His professor had asked each student to pretend that they were living their last day on earth: If they had the chance to write one letter to one person, to whom would it be and what would it say? Joel, still shaken, professed that he loved both me and John equally, but with only one letter permitted, he had written it to me because, "I know I was not an easy child growing up. Thank you for always standing by me and never giving up on me no matter how hard I made it." My heart skipped a beat. My kneejerk reaction was to say that was what parents did. But what brought me to tears was what followed, "My wish is that I will be as strong and as patient with my children when I have them." Needless to say, we were both in tears.

Along with Joel's passion and commitment to what he loved, a tad of distraction also hung on. That, in part, resulted in a double senior year. He had forgotten about the foreign language requirement, two classes that could not be taken in parallel. Remaining at the university full time also allowed him to enroll in supplementary economics classes of interest to him.

After attaining his degree in Economics, Joel stayed in Richmond where he began a career in sales which suited his sociable personality perfectly. As an ardent worker, he poured his heart and soul into his job. The distance between us was only an hour and a half by car. In his free time, he remained an avid cyclist on a team sponsored by a local sport shop. When he raced in our area, we sometimes had opportunities to host his teammates which allowed us to get to know them as well. His passion for cycling nourished his dream to someday open a bicycle shop.

We were all extremely proud of our children who were all grown and creating their own paths to their own futures. Elisa's daughter, Jennifer had a dual degree in education and psychology from Shippensburg University. She taught elementary school then a change of career led her to nursing school. Today she is employed as a delivery nurse at the same hospital that Pop was cared for. She also kicked off a new generation with the birth of Zander and Haiti.

Her sister, Jacelyn, fulfilled her dream to pursue dancing. It was an incredible accomplishment. Before starting senior year in high school, she had been the victim of a horrific car accident. The car, barreling several times, stabilized upside down in a corn field. She was still inside the vehicle with one arm outside the window, pinned underneath the car. The rain-soaked ground allowed her arm to sink and avoid being crushed. Her serious neck injuries required multiple surgeries and wearing a halo for a good portion of her senior year. As she recovered, she was told she would never dance again. Determined, despite her pain, she performed beautifully, moving all of the spectators to tears in her senior recital. Not too interested in the academics, she took a break from her university. After that, she was accepted in the field she loved at the California Institute of the Arts where she graduated with dual degrees: Dance and photography. As dancing turned more taxing on her injuries, she pursued a Master's Degree in Dance Therapy that followed with her doctorate.

Alfredo's son, Michael, grew up to be a handsome young man. He retained his same massive amount of energy. He studied Political Science and International Relations at Saint Joseph's University. He completed his graduate studies at the University of Pittsburgh in Public and International Affairs of Security and Intelligence. Employment opportunities moved him near us. He also became an avid cyclist and devoted much of his time to cycling, training and racing.

Gino's boys, Andrew and Nicholas, both played music and football in school. Andrew pursued his passion for trains. He became certified in railway engineering and conducted freight trains. Nicholas was the only blonde born in our family. After high school, he enlisted in the United States Marine Corps for eight years to serve our country. His post was mostly in Information Technology. After his service, he returned to civilian life and continued in the same line of work. My brother's youngest daughter, Makenna, was beautiful, bright and talented. She loved the outdoors and revealed a great talent in the artistic field. After high school, she went on to study nursing. In their spare time, all three children help their father at the bar. All of our children had grown up to be grounded and responsible human beings.

As parents, we certainly had not always made the best choices and had made our share of mistakes. However, what was clear and beyond any shadow of doubt was that, like my parents, our hearts were full of pride when it came to our children. My affirmation came on more than one occasion as our son confidently articulated, "I am in a good place...I am fortunate to have parents who gave me a strong foundation and gave me the tools to make good choices in life..." Also in my heart, was an awareness that it was because of our parents and their sacrifices that we were able to give and do for our children, what they could not do for us.

9

A calling to the Nord

The children were on their path to their own lives. Our daughter and her husband settled nearby. Danielle taught at an elementary school while continuing to take additional enrichment and specialty classes in her field. She and Ryan bought a home nearby and took on several home improvement projects. They devoted their time between work, family, friends, their little family of furry pets and they ran marathons. Joel remained in his college town where he bought his first home. It had been newly renovated while it also preserved its original character of the early 1920s. Noticing the recess, evidence that once allowed coal to be shoveled in its basement, made me smile. As with many older dwellings, something was always in need of repair. It was not uncommon to find Joel and John on FaceTime working through fixing one thing or another. Joel had turned into quite the handyman and was always ready to tackle new projects. There, he lived with his very lovely and kindhearted life partner, Harper, who also shared his love for the outdoors and furry friends. Joel was very passionate about his work and stayed active in the cycling community. He and Harper also incorporated furry rescues in their lives. All the furry cousins were friends. Accordingly, when they visited all together, the pack took over our yard and had no need for humans.

Life changed as we all branched off in different directions while our family bond never wavered. The things that were important to us remained the same. Even as our children went about their business, they kept the spirit of family. For many years to come, our daughter still talked about Uncle Gino's six o'clock in the morning stopover to share a cup of coffee. For a while, it was the only free time that my little brother could visit because of his heavy work schedule. We always found the way to one another.

For our little family, annual vacations together remained sacred. Between children, nephew and friends, we had a full table for most Sunday meals. Major holidays were dedicated to the extended family to which future generations synched up for the pleasure of all being together. Even with the protests over the strong aroma of the baccala that lingered in the house for days, it was not Christmas Eve without it. Dominic and I typically took charge of frying it in the basement to eliminate the problematic odor and to protect it from banishment. The first piece was always shared among the chefs as it exited the frying pan.

With both of our own children settled, John and I talked more seriously about retirement. He was our master behind planning to comfortably leave our jobs earlier in life to do more meaningful things, or simply put, to do what we want, when we want! In that vein, by late 2012, John took an opportunity when his company incentivized employees with their decision to downsize. Between a love for golf, volunteering on the golf course and woodworking projects, John's intended few months off grew into full retirement.

My days needed to be fuller at that point in my life, so I stayed in my job. Work projects were demanding which suited me. Interestingly, our empty nest was something that I had expected to be a more difficult adjustment. It was not my problem. Staying busy was in response to escaping uninvited thoughts linked to the horrific nightmare of April 16th. Work gave me little time to dwell in my private thoughts. My thirtyish minute commute to work that had once served to plan out the day in my head, started to feel longer as the emotional rollercoaster of 2006 and 2007 began to catch up with me. Time had passed and changed my emotions but the aching and raw pain lingered. Certain times of the year were always harder and more reflective. A cell phone that in the past had been a luxury was now a necessity. It was always by my side, charged and on my night stand during the night, just in case the children called. All of their calls were answered to make sure that all was OK. If my calls didn't immediately reach them, my throat tightened until they answered, then I pretended everything was fine. Clumsily, I tried to conceal my worry. Without a doubt, that tragedy had left me borderline paranoid.

On most days, I gathered up enough strength to push away the tears and replace them with good memories as my mind flashed to young Joel walking out of his bedroom with socks and sandals. I saw Joel shedding real tears as he tried to convince me that he could not complete a first grade homework assignment because his brain worked differently, it was not made for that kind of work. I saw Joel graduate from college. I saw Danielle in pigtails jumping on her bed. I saw her as a school teacher. I saw her sitting with her brother in a cardboard box, giggling. I saw a lifetime of happiness. I was very proud of the caring human beings that they had become. Being a mother to them was, by far, the greatest joy of my existence.

As my mind wandered through laughter over a science experiment involving weeks of bananas rotting in our basement that Danielle and Mary had worked on, the tears welled. Opening the bedroom door to find two high school girls jumping on the bed or mimicking their infamous fish faces and giggling, sometimes also carried me back to those darker days.

What floated here and there, was a simpler life of the days gone by in the Nord of France. Glimpses of yesteryear created an escape path. In my mind, I ran alongside a fence then crossed a field of potatoes to my kindergarten, I played hide and seek on our street in *Fenain* or waved to my parents leaning against the wooden shutters as they chatted with neighbors. I let the wind softly blow on my face as I peeked around Elisa from the back of her bicycle. As more and more of those happier childhood memories surfaced, my mind sidetracked to ancient chats with Pop when I should have been more inquisitive. I wondered what had become of our neighbors, friends and a community so much a part of our lives a half century ago. Pop had kept informed over the years, then those letters slowly dwindled as his friends, one by one, lost their own battle to health problems linked with laboring in the coal mine.

My young school friends in the Nord, Nadine and Danila, that I had separated from at the age of nine reappeared in my mind. After a few years, a sluggish communication eventually faded along with my French. Sometimes, Elisa and I had spoken French with one another to keep our conversations private, but it was soon completely replaced with English and Italian so we could more easily fit into our community and, at the same time, converse with our grandparents who spoke very little English. I thought about my unsuccessful attempts to find my old friends even in the recent years.

Pondering on our uprooting, Pop's bravery to displace our family not only once, but twice came to my mind. First, by saving us from the misery in the fields of Southern Italy, then again from the brutal depths of the mines of the Nord that led us to our final destination in the land of opportunity. With his work at the mine, he was able to save enough money for us to buy our first house when we arrived in America, the place where each of us was able to build our own future.

Those deep-rooted memories drove me to searching other avenues that unearthed only tidbits of information related to the town of *Fenain*. The name of the coal mine where Pop had worked did not immediately come to mind. Everyone had always referred to it as "*la fosse*" which was the French word for the mine. Eventually, I came across a reference to a coal mine company in the Nord called *Anzin*. Scrolling through their extensive list of mines, *fosse Agache* and *fosse Heurteau* instantly awakened my memories.

141

Using the internet and thanks to satellite street views, *Fenain* came to life. Wandering through the town on my computer screen, confirmed that our old neighborhood was still very much alive in my memory, making our home at 3 *Rue Taffin* very easy to find. Zooming in was bittersweet. The house looked exactly the same! The road was now paved and the large metal gate protecting the tall black mountain at the end of our street was gone. Also missing, was the country kitchen that once faced Mamouch's living room. Completely absorbed, I "walked" through town searching for my school, *Ecole des Tilleuls*, and the homes of my friends but those aerial views were unavailable.

Several old pictures of the black mountain, our community neighboring the mine and my elementary school in *Fenain* popped up online. A newspaper article explained that my school had been torn down and replaced by a new one. The pictures of the mine *Agache* were old aerial views taken in the early 1960s. They looked exactly as I remembered them. A few articles that talked about the closing of the coal mine of *Agache* in 1976 left me wondering about what had happened to our neighbors and friends. All of my treasures were printed and shared with my family so that they had visuals to connect with my stories.

The search for our home in *City Heurteau* was less fruitful. Other than the photo of us at the front door, one on the back porch and my memory of our home's surroundings, there was nothing else. What little documentation Pop had saved was not easily accessible and no one seemed to remember our address.

A few months later, I recalled that *City Heurteau* was near a place called *Hornaing*. I redirected my search there once I figured out the correct spelling of the city. My first hit on *Hornaing* was so phenomenal, my feet were already doing a happy dance while my brain was catching up to fully grasp what my eyes were seeing. It was the enormous refrigerant associated with La Centrale, a daily view from my early childhood which was still deeply rooted in my memories. There it was, before my eyes in this aerial view displayed on my computer screen. Catching my breath, remembering my way home from school with respect to those refrigerants, I "walked" in that direction. We lived on the last street which was separated from the pasture by a trail to the woods.

With almost fifty years gone by, was it possible that our house or the pasture was still there? It was so vivid in my memory, as was the home of Alfredo's godmother across the street, as was the tower and the garages along the path to my kindergarten. It did not take long to find my school and a pot of gold. Seeing myself in the pasture again, picking buttercups and laying in the grass contemplating the universe, even without an address, there was no mistaking our home! It was confirmed after showing it to Mom and Elisa. They now they remembered *Rue de Donzere*.

An incredible feeling drove me to search for everything possible about my childhood place that held so many magnificent memories. During my internet travel, I stumbled upon *Memoir of a child of the Nord: Hornaing 1950 - 1960* by Jacques Pagniez. It seemed almost unbelievable to discover a book written about this tiny place of long ago, a place that unmistakably had special meaning to someone else too. My fingers trembled with excitement navigating through the website. The years that the author wrote about corresponded, more or less, to the same time that our family had lived there. I didn't recognize his name and while he wrote of *Hornaing* and our home was in *City Heurteau*, perhaps our paths crossed at the open market.

My initial search for Jacques Pagniez resulted in an obituary. Rejecting the idea that this was the end of the line, I pressed on and discovered another mention of that name affiliated with Lire Autrement[27] in Paris. Although it was late, I wrote an email via their website in the hope that it would be routed to Mr. Pagniez and that he was the right person. After introducing myself, I asked for guidance on where to find more information about *City Heurteau.*

Needless to say, I was late for work the following morning because I was soaking in the joy of reading and rereading a heartwarming email response by Mr. Pagniez. Included were several photos of an older *Hornaing* such as the chateau of the Baronne in the forest near our house. My eyes welled in recognition of the images of the big church, the *fosse Heurteau* and Elisa's school that I had frequented on the back of her bike.

A new friendship was born with a fellow Hornaingian, Jacques Pagniez and *Memoirs of a Child of the Nord* evolved into my calling to the Nord of France.

---

[27] Lire Autrement: Founded in 2001 by Simone Herault. A company of public readings and animations accompanied by professional comedians and musicians.

10

Meeting a fellow "child of the Nord"

Completely enthralled with my new treasure, *Memoirs of a Child of the Nord*, I discovered so much more than even imagined. Jacques and I were only a few years apart with an overlap in the Nord by only a year. Yet, we shared an abundance of comparable fond memories around our family, bicycles, the *ducasse* and outings into the forest. Emotions simply overflowed each time another flash of my own childhood was re-experienced. As some memories became more vivid, other fragments began to the take more shape. His story not only awakened, it revealed more precise or missing details about my own life.

Learning more about the environment in which we had lived so long ago, the chapter, *Hornaing* par *Marchienne* (Nord), became a bit of a history lesson for me. No doubt the town had at least as much history as the little village of *Orsara* where each of the walls and streets had voices of their own. It was also the moment that I realized my family lived in a *coron*, and that *City Heurteau* was not the city that I had known it to be my entire life.

A *coron* was one of many small communities of almost identical homes built by the *Anzin* coal mine company to accommodate their workers and the arrival of people like us, foreign laborers. The homes were situated close to the mine so workers could live with their families while easily getting to their place of employment on foot or by taking a company shuttle. The *coron* of *City Heurteau* was situated on the other side of the railroad tracks at the extreme north of *Hornaing*.

As the puzzle pieced together, I fully grasped that our family had lived in two of the many *corons* of the Nord: one in *Hornaing* and one in *Fenain*. The names of the *corons* were different but they all had the same décor: a mine, a black mountain, a self-contained community and many desperate people looking for a way to put food on the table for their families. What remained true for me, was that our home in the *coron* of *City Heurteau* was our first link to a chain of events for a chance at a better life. In my childhood, *City Heurteau* had always felt like a big place with a school, the chapel and a grocer who were all somehow affiliated with either the mine or the Centrale power plant. Above all, I remembered a warm and welcoming community where everyone knew and helped one another.

The tall headframes surrounded by a fence seen daily from our front door, played a significant role in the mine. Those headframes that I had dubbed as the Eiffel Towers so long ago, held cages that served as "elevators" to descend men, squeezed together, four to six hundred feet deep into the earth. It was fascinating to read that those mine pits had been used as refuge for the inhabitants of *Hornaing* during the bombings of the war from 1939 to 1945.

The book guided me to other resources for information about where we had lived. The mine and the *coron of City Heurteau* in *Hornaing* were named in memory of Emil Heurteau, an engineer commissioned by the company of *Anzin* to modernize their mine. Heurteau was their last mine established in 1927. No coal was ever mined in *Heurteau* which explained never seeing workers around those buildings. Additionally, Pop's story about the two pits of this mine serving for ventilation of the *fosse Agache* at *Fenain* made more sense to me. The large brick building on my path to kindergarten was the coal power plant, the Centrale. It had replaced much of the mine surface in 1958, the year before we arrived to *City Heurteau*.

The railroad track, always emphatically forbidden for me to cross, connected *fosse Heurteau* with *fosse Agache* in *Fenain*. That track ran side by side to another line, the first international connection between Paris and Brussels which also served the city of *Douai*.

In Jacques' writing about the Grand Place where all the traditional holidays took place, he evoked a memory that had fused together the events occurring around Bastille Day: the *ducasse*, and the distribution of scholastic awards. Since those events were all so close together, around the 14th of July and always at the same place, I mistakenly recalled them as one affair. As more precise moments resurfaced, I laughed out loud thinking about the *ducasse* near the *Heurteau Chapel* with Elisa, me attached to one hand and the rooster in the other. The entire scene with the rooster trying to escape his fate next to the roasted potatoes the following Sunday was reborn in my memory.

The *ducasse* and the distribution of awards of *Fenain* were even more vivid in my mind. Closing my eyes, the excitement as Elisa and Pop held my hand on our way to the fairgrounds came to life, the smell of cotton candy still reached my nostrils, and the laughter rang in my head recalling our walks around the grounds, not to mention being relentless about riding bumper cars. Sometimes, Elisa took me home from the *ducasse* and returned later with her friends. Years later, Elisa confessed to sneaking into a striptease tent with a few of her friends. One friend, who was on his way into the seminary, acted as their escort and guarantor of their morality!

The distribution of the school prizes which also ensued around this time, always brought a warm smile to our family. I recalled Pop's proud look when my name was called for my precious books. I so missed his crooked smile and wink, with his head slightly bent to the left. I chuckled as I remembered hiding my book, *Tale of the bright island* inside the crate that we had shipped when we departed for America, a treasure still found on my bookshelf forever after.

Thinking about the forest near *City Heurteau*, I imagined those olden days when Pop hopelessly tried to teach Mom to ride a bicycle. The picnics in the forest came to life as I inhaled the perfume of the lily of the valley or sitting in the grass eating a sandwich with butter and a little jam that we had stuffed in the sack on the back of Elisa's bicycle. Even more vivid was our family Sunday dinners which were followed by afternoon adventures on Pop's mobylette or card games.

As more precise memories came back to life, it helped to reconnect more pieces of the puzzle of my life. It occurred to me that the weekly show that we stood in line for at the home of Madame Bonzanini on *Rue Taffin* was called *La Piste aux Etoiles*. It was a magnificent spectacle of clowns, trapeze, acrobats, animals and magicians. That exceptionally popular circus on black and white television, attracted children and adults alike who congregated at homes of those rare friends or neighbors who possessed a television.

The connection to our roots bonded a very special friendship with Jacques. We began to correspond more frequently and talked about our past and present life. With the avalanche of stories to share with my family over Sunday dinners, the joy I felt about this new connection to my past was apparent. Yet, I was caught off-guard when Danielle and John proposed a trip to the Nord. That idea had never occurred to me. They countered with, "What was the point of the research, if not to return." To that argument, I had no explanation that could easily be put into words.

What I did know, was that reading *Memoire of a child of the Nord: Hornaing* had been a breath of fresh air. It added authenticity to a deep and distant life that never left my heart. Simply overwhelmed by a multitude of emotions, a part of me wanted to touch and feel some of those memories again, however, my feelings remained mixed when it came to going back to the Nord. Associating the Nord with the mine that had taken Pop's life far too soon, I felt guilt-stricken to see those years as the happiest of my childhood memories. Also knowing that almost fifty years later, the Nord was a different place from what we had left behind, I wanted to preserve my fond memories. So for the moment, I somewhat ignored the idea.

Thinking on the subject more deeply, our homes were there, the towns were obviously there, the mine was not and, most likely, neither were our friends. If I were to go back, I would want to share the adventure with my sister, John and my children. Recognizing that was not possible for various reasons, my attention turned to Elisa since the pair of us had the most passionate connections to the Nord. The idea began to sound a little less crazy.

Upon asking Elisa to join me on a journey to our Nord, she reminded me of the obvious. The ordeal of leaving at seventeen years old had been enormously difficult for her. I agreed that going back was hard. At the same time, many memories of the Nord were very rich for both of us. The two of us could relive a part of that together. I requested that she consider it before quickly saying no and I would respect her decision. Already aware of her response since she hadn't brought up the subject for an exceedingly long time, I asked. She expressed that going back was still too hard.

Unsure that it was something John was interested in doing, I asked anyway. He replied without hesitation, "Seriously, what are you thinking…of course I'm going with you."

To make this decision real, I shared my thoughts with Jacques. *Memoire of a child of the Nord: Hornaing* had been such a profound inspiration to me, we were thinking of making a trip…So, I had decided, it was real!

11

Birth of a dream

Obviously, this excursion would be incomplete without meeting the person whose writing brought my days of strolling at the open market at the Grand Place, the bicycle rides into the forest and my olden school days back to life. His heartwarming response put me over the moon: "I am delighted that my childhood memories revived yours and I am delighted with your magnificent idea of returning to France to retrace the steps of your young years." He not only intended to meet us in Paris, but he enthusiastically offered to guide us on the journey down memory lane in *Hornaing* and *Fenain*. His kindness and generosity was beyond imagination. Words were not sufficient to describe the euphoria of this fairytale that left me floating on fluffy clouds. I wanted to preciously preserve that magical sensation.

Regrettably, that anticipated journey was hindered due to work commitments. We were awaiting the release of a formal government request to bid for follow-on work to one of our contracts that was coming to an end. As the program manager for that project, I felt obligated to wait and, to be fair, I had not shared my travel desires with the company. After waiting for an entire year, the imminent government request for proposal still had not arrived, so John and I picked a date and purchased our airline tickets. If necessary, my computer would accompany me to France. Although that was not an ideal choice, it was certainly not the first or last time that my vacation included work. I had always done what was necessary to make it work. So our adventure to the Nord was set for spring 2015.

Once Jacques received confirmation for the trip, he set a train in motion that moved faster than the speed of light. In his endless charm, he suggested, "We can journey from Paris to Lille by train, then rent a car for an adventure to retrace our childhood steps."

Jacques posed various email inquiries to better prepare for our visit. They revolved around our time in the Nord: where we had lived, about my family and their work, what originally brought us to France, names of our schools, and some photos both old and new. In the course of our correspondence, he sent me various photos. One in particular was a lantern that the coal miners had used long ago. My heart simply sank. Although we had always known Pop worked hard, he rarely spoke of it. On the other hand, telling us of being two thousand feet deep into the earth, day after day, with a pickaxe should have been sufficient for us to understand. I remembered how terrifying it was for himself and us to not recognize him on the few occasions that he did not shower at work. Knowing Pop who always tried to protect us, there was no doubt that withholding the details of his work was likely deliberate. What I understood more and more, was his desire to be outside in the sunlight piddling in the yard, or taking us on Sunday afternoon rides on his mobylette.

Being curious, naturally I began to wonder about Jacques' planning. But this time the curiosity was locked away, allowing myself to be guided by the unknown. Completely out of character, my typical millions of questions went unasked. In that vein, I prepared an abridged summary of our background: A little about our family and our origin in the small village of *Orsara* in Southern Italy.

Additionally, I evoked my regrets about losing contact with my young school friends in *Fenain* and my failed attempts to find them in the recent years. I also mentioned our second migration to America in November 1966 and that, sadly, Pop had been lost to silicosis in October 2006. As for his request for old photos, we only had a handful.

Jacques managed everything in secret, leaving breadcrumbs here and there that hinted at an exceptional adventure. He left me speechless and overawed with emotion with his note that "the mayors and several friends in *Hornaing* and *Fenain* were helping to organize a homecoming to rediscover your childhood memories." I had to reread his message to ensure my translation from French was correct.

Jacques communicated that everything was in place for March 26, 2015, amplifying that, "It will be a long day, rich in discovery and emotion." What he did not know, was that I was already in an extraordinary emotional trance.

Like a child in front of a box that I was not allowed to open, it was total enchantment! With one foot already inside this fairytale, I did not want to awaken. Instead, I put my other foot into the cloud and let myself be carried. Sometimes I had to pinch myself to ensure that I was not asleep. There was no doubt that fireworks of all colors were popping up around me. I was not sure what we would find in the Nord after almost fifty years, but it would be positively divine!

With our reunion a week away, my emotions were out of control. I could no longer wait to touch, feel and walk that path of my childhood. To avoid from immersing completely in this fairyland, I stayed busy at work. The request for proposal was finally released. It turned out to be perfect timing as it kept me occupied. Our work was completed in the late hours on the day prior to our trip, leaving my mind completely free to immerse in my dream and embark on the next phase of a fantastic fairytale.

There was little time to pack before Danielle and Ryan arrived to take us to the airport. We took a little detour on the way to celebrate a belated birthday lunch for Ryan at one of his favorite Thai restaurants. Then, we boarded our twilight flight that had a stopover in Iceland where we expected to spend a few days on the return trip.

Since we both loved cultural and historical excursions, what better place to be than Paris on the banks of the Seine and its picturesque streets. It was John's first time in France. My only visit to Paris was our family journey to the American Embassy for our formalities to depart for America in the summer of 1966.

Jacques and his warm smile greeted us at the entrance of the terminal of the Paris - Charles De Gaulle Airport. Luckily, he was an expert on the train system. There was no doubt that without him, we would still be lost somewhere between the three trains and two transfers. We dropped off our bags in our tiny apartment on Rue Pierre Premier de Serbie, perfectly situated midway between the Arc of Triumph and the Eiffel Tower. An added bonus for us was the huge open market directly behind the building two days per week.

With restaurants everywhere, we simply crossed our street to a brasserie and grabbed a quick lunch with Jacques in an air of already knowing one another for a lifetime. Later that evening, we met Jacques and his friend, Simone for dinner. Jacques understood more English than he admitted and Simone's was perfect, making our chats about everything and nothing flow very easily.

Jacques' excitement regarding our fabulous adventure was obvious. He transformed into a little boy as he enthusiastically talked about our journey. I glimpsed Simone prompting him that the plans were still "top secret," when his efforts to contain himself began to fall short. He swiftly pulled his hand over his mouth to keep the words from spilling out, then finally said, "You will cry." He did not know that the tears were already difficult to keep at bay.

After dinner, we dillydallied a bit on our walk back because Simone had reserved a surprise for us. We had to laugh as we admitted to one another that we could not possibly walk any slower. We finally stopped as Simone kept eyeing the time. Then, with all its splendor, the Eiffel Tower adorned with bright blinking lights magically came to life. It was the perfect end to a perfect day!

Despite Jacques' busy schedule, he guided us through the quaint streets in Montmartre on one of the wettest days of the year in Paris. Entirely soaked, we toured Sacre Coeur and Place de Tertre where, on drier days, artists set up their easels and hung their work on a clothesline for tourists. Jacques pointed out a tiny patch of a vineyard on Rue Saint-Vincent, a hidden treasure in Paris that yielded about five hundred liters of wine per year. Another interesting find was the home of Dalida, whom my parents adored.

We slipped into Les Deux Moulins Café, in part, to escape the rain. To our disappointment the café was not yet open for business. After Jacques privately spoke with the manager, he led us to a table where we were served coffee. There, Jacques and John had a profound heart-to-heart about Cognac versus Armagnac. On our way back, we stopped at Jacques' favorite liquor store where John indulged in a Cognac-Armagnac tasting. Suffice it to say that while I eyed the shelves full of bottles of champagne, John was already cradling Armagnac like a baby in his arms.

At the end of this rich and eventful day, we confirmed our plans to meet at the train station in Paris, La Gare du Nord, at six o'clock in the morning on Wednesday for our adventure to *Hornaing* and *Fenain*.

12

Homecoming

The butterflies fluttering in my stomach along with the insomnia marked the arrival of the long anticipated journey to the Nord. A day that had been already perfect from its inception and for which its details were still secret. Simone collected us at our apartment by taxi since no one wanted to risk John or me missing our early departure from the Gare du Nord. Jacques, wearing a complicit smile, met us on the station platform. The gap in a small white paper bag that he so carefully carried, filled the air with a similar aroma as the bread truck of yesteryear when it turned the corner of our street. Sinking my teeth into that freshly baked chocolate croissant was a walk in the majestic past on *Rue Taffin*.

Jacques and Simone had packed a few distractions for the hour long train ride to Lille. Knowing my love for reading, Jacques included a few treasures for my return to America. The stash included *GRACE A MA VOIX*, a work about the dynamic "voice of the trains" in France, Simone. The paperbacks on cheeses and sweets of the Nord made me chuckle because he had clearly discovered some of my biggest weaknesses.

The selection included a work by Marinelli. It was about Italians who had escaped the misery of their native land in a sunny Southern Italy for the darkness at the foot of tall dark mounds of coal waste in the mines of Northern France during the 1900s. While they all had stories of their own, they all shared a forced departure by men who needed to feed their families. Like our family, many intended to leave Italy temporarily, earn some money, then reunite with their families where they could buy some land to build a better life. But for many different reasons, most never went back.

Knowing my deep interest in regard to the mines of the French department of the Nord, Jacques incorporated some of his other works, *The Three Ages of the Mine* and *Rails of the Nord* which covered some history and context of the mines in the Nord. It told the how and the why the *Anzin* Company constructed the communities for the families of the mine such as ours. Essentially, it was in response to improve the dangerous working and living conditions well described in Zola's *Germinal*. The work was still dangerous but the benefits were far better for those who were in need. Families were able to live together in a home provided by the company in an infrastructure that included medical care, heat, education for the children and a place of worship. The type and size of housing allowance depended on the position held at the mine.

Nearing *Douai*, Jacques signaled that we were approaching one of the last standing mounds of coal waste in the Nord. Given that it would be dark for our return trip late in the evening, I didn't want to miss what could be my only chance to see it. Pensive and serene, my eyes were glued to the glass. Occasionally, they closed to hold back the tears. My hands stayed firmly tucked under my legs to keep them from trembling.

As the train made its turn around the right of the tall mound, I imagined the black mountain of *Agache* in *Fenain* from my childhood that had left a similar knot in the pit of my stomach. My mind rewound to Pop entering through our blue wooden gate where my little brothers and I eagerly awaited. Then all three of us ran into his arms to kiss him. Smiling, I closed my eyes again to invite more memories to float through my thoughts.

In Lille, we picked up our rental car and drove toward *Hornaing*. We had all hoped for a warm spring day, instead, it was cold, damp and probably more aligned with the depressing weather of the Nord that I had experienced as a child. For the next forty-five minutes, we passed signs of the towns familiar in my memory, *Roubaix, Douais, Escaudain, Somain* and *Fenain*.

In *Hornaing*, we made a short stop at Jacques' childhood home on *Rue Wilson*. The sidewalk across the street with its tall wall had not changed from the view of fifty years earlier depicted on the front cover of his book revealing young Jacques in shorts standing alongside his bicycle. It seemed fitting to begin our tour there since Jacques' work had been so significant in reviving my memories.

In transit to the school where Elisa had graduated, the overpowering presence of the gigantic refrigerants, all still intact, were hard to miss. It was *City Heurteau*. Minutes later, my attention moved to the parking lot of my sister's old school where the doors of multiple vehicles filled with people, flew open. Waiting for us in the bitter cold was the welcoming committee! It was beyond anything we could have imagined, naturally, John and I were speechless.

Amid the crowd that had helped to coordinate the top-secret event, were a photographer and a journalist from the regional daily newspaper, *La Voix du Nord*. There were also representatives from the Historic Museum of *Fenain* and a retired English teacher who served as an interpreter for the occasion. A bell rang in hearing the interpreter's name, Mr. Lebon, prompting me to ask if his mother had also been a teacher. As it turned out, she was one of Elisa's teachers as well as a principal for my kindergarten. She almost certainly was the influential force for me to attend school regularly. Mrs. Lebon was now deceased, but what an honor it was to be able to tell her son how much she meant to me and my sister.

The present-day principal of the school arrived soon after. We began with a tour of the now enlarged co-ed school. Behind Elisa's bike as a little girl, my view had been from afar, usually beside the large metal gate at the entrance into the courtyard. A heaviness in my heart reminded me of how much I wished that my sister had been by my side to walk where she had walked so long ago.

Settling into one of the classrooms in the original part of the school that was now second grade, we talked with the students about the adventure to "my home" as a little girl of some fifty years prior. Some were astonished to hear that their school had once been an all-girl school, others were suspicious of persons resembling their grandparents claiming to once being children themselves.

Cozying into a tiny desk next to an adorable little girl, we both laughed at my attempt to read the book in her hand, *Marie en Amazonie* by Christian Lamblin and François Roudot in my now very broken French. It highlighted the mentions here and there upon our return to the Nord, that we were "the Americans." It amusingly carried me back to the olden days, reminding me of our visits to *Orsara* in my very early years, where we were "the French." Upon our arrival in America, we were "the Italians." Breaking my concentration nearby, someone joked about the size of the chair but being just under five feet tall, the fit was perfect.

The Town Hall of *Hornaing* to meet the Mayor was our next stop. Our introduction evolved into a fabulous surprise. Opening their thick double doors revealed a reception hall full of guests with Mayor Delannoy in full ceremonial dress. Glassy eyed, trembling knees slowly moved me forward in total disbelief. We were surrounded by friends of our family from a lifetime ago in *City Heurteau*. John and I found ourselves speechless again, an apparent recurrence for that day! Even their tables were charmingly adorned with fresh flowers and refreshments alongside countless bottles of champagne atop of snowy white tablecloths.

Among the guests was Jeanine, the sweet young girl who, many years ago, spent time with me after school. She remembered the rides to the big church in

Hornaing and our afternoon chitchats on our front steps with my mom and baby Alfredo. The family who owned the farm near the railroad tracks, who once deposited milk on our window sill daily, was also present. With Mrs. Decomier, we reminisced about Mom's visits to their farm to buy cheese. It was hard not to chuckle as it brought to mind our genuine dilemma to be fresh out of Romano or parmesan since it topped off nearly every dish of pasta that we ate. Mom and Pop had also left their imprint at the Dancing Café. The once young owner of the café, who was among the guests, vividly remembered the king and queen of the dance floor. Uncertain about how the day would unfold, we were suddenly elated to have brought a hodge-podge of family photos that had covered more or less fifty years.

Entirely dazed, John and I made our way around this magnificent crowd. In a corner of the hall, a gentleman was talking on his cell phone for quite some time. When we had an opportunity to speak, he confessed to conversing with his wife to ensure the details of the story were accurate, then he proceeded to tell me an amazing story about Pop.

Back in our days in *City Heurteau*, his wife's family lived just a few doors from ours. Some of the finer details were a bit fuzzy but in essence, when his father-in-law had died suddenly, the mine would not pay for the burial which, in turn, left a huge unexpected financial burden for the family. Pop must have been severely distressed by that situation because he discretely organized a collection among friends, neighbors and colleagues. Additionally, he arranged and assisted with making needed repairs to their home along with other preparations prior to the funeral service.

That gentleman disclosed that he had come to represent his family because they will never forget what Pop had done for them, without his involvement, the family would not have been able to give his father-in-law a proper burial. It was not a story that I had previously heard, yet it did not surprise me. Pop was Pop. He did things for others and never talked about them. That day, it was I, his daughter, who wore the proud look on my face.

A soft tap on my shoulder shed more light on the nature of Jacques' questions in the early preparation for our visit. We all turned our eyes to Mayor Delannoy who, in perfect English, recited:

"There once was a little Italian girl named Olga Russo...The Russo family lived in Orsara, province of Foggia in Italy prior to moving in the commune of Hornaing in 1959.
Everything started in 1958 when your father, Michelino, decided to leave Italy to feed his family that was confronted with difficult hardships. He worked in the mine of Agache in Fenain.

156

In 1959, your father decided to uproot your family in France soon after the death of your brother. Your father, your mother, your older sister Elisa and you moved to the City Heurteau at 59 Rue de Donzere.

Olga, you attended kindergarten at Suzanne Lanoy situated on Rue d'Arles, your sister at the school for girls (you will revisit your school and the street where you have lived this afternoon).

In 1961, the family grew with the birth of your brother Alfredo then another brother, Gino, in 1963.

In 1963 at the age of 6, your father decided to move the family to Fenain on Rue Taffin to shorten his commute to the mine. There you attended the School of Tilleuls.

Then in 1966, you left France for America.

You have cherished your memories with wonderful souvenirs of Hornaing, especially the ducasse, the distribution of the school awards, your afternoons and evenings in the garden and all your neighbors united...

It has been 48 years that you are in America, near Washington, DC.

And here you are making a special journey, a voyage at the heart of your childhood to revisit places where you have lived, gone to school...I hope that we have helped you find and retrace all of your important moments of your life in the commune of Hornaing."

The tears were getting more and more difficult to hold back as Mayor Delannoy presented me with several gifts: Alfredo's birth announcement as he was born in *City Heurteau,* a decorative crystal plate of *Hornaing* and a medal of the city. Included with these treasures were photographs of *Hornaing* of yesterday and today depicting places that had significant connections to my childhood.

When my words sounded audible again, I addressed the mayor and the guests. Mr. Lebon was usually nearby to save me from my broken French, yet, both he and Jacques encouraged me to speak in French. No matter how mishmashed it was, I knew what it meant to them and what was in my heart. So, I continued:

"...All my appreciation for the warmest welcome that is beyond anything I ever imagined. So many of my childhood memories have a very special place in my heart. They are wonderful memories. I am proud to be here after all these years. I want to honor Pop and more than anything, I wish that he too could be here. I know he is proudly smiling over us. Both he and Mom would have been very proud and happy to see their friends here. Anyone who knew Pop knew he loved to talk, a lot! But, there are also so many big things he did not share with us. My only regret is that I did not ask him more questions

157

about the Nord and the mine because between his love to tell stories and the right questions, I'd understand so much more.

...Naturally, finding Jacques' book of Hornaing put this dream into motion...what a treasure to find his book...who writes about this little place of Hornaing? Clearly, it is a place that has special meaning to others too. So, it is all thanks to Jacques inspiration and his book that I am here today. Thank you!"

Hopeful that all of my sentiments were adequately conveyed in my *frenglish*, I was sure that they understood what was in my heart more than what was said.

Seeing our neighborhood friends was incredibly moving. John took charge of exchanging addresses in advance of some difficult goodbyes. Our next stopovers were my kindergarten and "home." Through the glass in the car, once again, my eyes walked to *Suzanne Lanoy* using my familiar landmarks, the giant refrigerant and the coal power plant. Entering my school onto soft carpeting immediately aired its warm ambiance. Several small wooden benches arranged in a circle replaced the long narrow tables and chairs of the old days.

Touring the rest of the school, we came upon several parent volunteers hard at work on a school fundraiser, stuffing candy in Easter baskets. Chatting here and there with some of the moms, I discovered that two of them were previous neighbors in *City Heurteau* who remembered Mom and Elisa well.

We lunched all together at *Suzanne Lanoy*. Beef, a traditional bean casserole of the Nord and, because we were in France, an enormous platter of French fries were served. As we were eating and chatting, we were also amused by the young children moving to and from their classes. They curiously peeked into the happenings of the lunchroom around a table completely filled with food, beer, wine and strange older people.

For our next stop at *Rue de Donzere*, my knees trembled even before arriving at the gate of our first family home in the Nord. Although everything was almost exactly the same, something felt a bit off. Standing directly in front of the house, it occurred to me that this was the house that I remembered as 57 not 59. It belonged to our neighbors whom Pop awakened and saved during the night of the fire. To my right, red and white bricks framed a door exactly as I remembered, but the stairs were missing. As I pondered, Jacques jumped beside me to knock on door number 57. The current residents welcomed us with open arms. My confusion was quickly resolved when I realized that the properties for 57 and 59 were now combined into a larger house. This was "home" after all! Obviously, the big coal stove no longer commanded the living room. What was surprising was my perception regarding the size of those rooms. In my child eyes, those tiny rooms once looked gigantic.

Before leaving for *Fenain*, we strolled to the end the road for a better view of the massive pasture where I too had left my scent during those glorious days of long ago. Jacques proposed that we stop to meet the farmers. When we arrived, Simone noticed that one of the calves was sick. She alerted the farmer who was not yet aware. We respectfully returned to our cars as, sadly, the family was making significantly difficult decisions at that time.

Arriving in *Fenain*, John knew my thoughts were with my childhood school friends. To distract me, he pointed out the electronic sign outside of the Town Hall welcoming *Olga Russo Waters from America to revisit Fenain*. Yet again, we were left breathless and wordless.

There, we met Madam Mayor Dupilet as well as several other members of the *Historical Society of Fenain*. A quick scan of the room confirmed that neither Danila nor Nadine were present. Resolving in my heart that I would never see them again, I continued to mingle with the guests around an equally bountiful spread of refreshments and champagne. Almost as quickly as Madam Mayor Dupilet launched into the formal portion of the ceremony, she unexpectedly stopped speaking. The entire room fell silent. Momentarily confused, my eyes followed those of the spectators to the back wall where they locked with those of someone who I instantly recognized.

Walking in what felt like slow motion towards her, all that rolled from my lips was, "Danila!" We fell into each other's arms, neither of us wanted to let go. A few whispers and chopped words between our tears might have been distinguishable. Still holding hands, when we finally came up for air, we noticed the guests standing around us were equally moved.

After we all collected ourselves, Madam Mayor Dupilet continued with the ceremony:

> *"My dear Olga…From our city council and our citizens, welcome to Fenain. It is a pleasure because many Fenainians habitants are of Italian origin. At that time, even the mayor, Gino Ferrari, was of Italian origin. It is an honor to see, fifty years later, the return of the little girl who never forgot where she came from."*

The Mayor's deeply touching words rang so true, I had never forgotten where I came from…nor did I want to. In response, similar sentiments to those earlier in the day at the Town Hall of *Hornaing* with respect to this incredible fairy tale were expressed. After we toasted with champagne, we circulated among our guests as Mrs. Bouriez, who had barely aged, entered the hall. I was simply over the moon knowing that Nadine could not be far behind. This was a dream come true!

159

During that deeply emotional reunion with Danila and Nadine, we reminisced about our old days together. So much had changed yet so much remained the same. In that moment, it did not feel like fifty years had passed. Furthermore, I did not mind departing for our next stop so quickly because my school friends joined us for the remainder of the day's adventure.

The three of us were elated for a school homecoming. A new modern school had recently replaced our old one. Our schoolyard, on the other hand, was relatively intact. There, in the spirit of school girls of yesteryear's *Ecole des Tilleuls*, we reminisced about our old days, the outside toilets, the fence that separated boys and girls while never forgetting our teachers: Madame Rudant and Madame Longelin.

From there, we convoyed to the terrain where the black mountain had once stood. Although a supermarket now sat on a large portion of the mine floor, *Fenain* had successfully preserved the ground that was once a giant heap of coal waste. Everyone who stood there that day was connected to that mine in one way or another. It was an extremely powerful feeling to stand on the now flat land alongside others who had husbands, fathers, brothers and sons with different stories but all the same, they had all sacrificed themselves in the coal mines that, in tandem, had nourished and plagued their families. The place where my father had given his life to save us from misery. Our collective pain as we thought about our loved ones who had labored it so, was all intertwined.

Taking full advantage of the darkness of nightfall to conceal my tears, I roamed hopelessly struggling to find a piece of coal that did not immediately disintegrate between my fingers. Guy Dionet, a member of the *Historic Society of Fenain* sensed my frustration. Tapping my shoulder, he whispered that a piece of coal had already been set aside for me, not to worry.

From the black mountain, we circled "home." After crossing the railroad tracks, the roof of our house on *Rue Taffin* was immediately visible even before turning the corner. Pointing out the grocer, Gernez, and the office of Dr. De La Robertie left Jacques somewhat stunned that I remembered such details. Apparently, Jacques' grandfather had the same doctor. It occurred to me that Dr. De La Robertie was employed by the coal mine company, serving all of the surrounding coal miners' communities.

When the mine closed around 1976, the mineworkers had been given the opportunity to purchase their home as Nadine's parents had opted. The remaining were sold to other buyers. The occupant of our old house was a former coal miner.

Turning onto *Rue Taffin* was beyond intense, butterflies fluttered in my belly when the current residents welcomed us with open arms. "My house" was almost intact. It was a bittersweet walk inside my heart that held so many of my best childhood memories. Climbing the staircase that once led me to the romance magazines under Mom and Pop's bed made me chuckle. The bedroom that Elisa and I had once shared was in the process of being remodeled. We laughed when I mentioned to the young woman who now occupied the room, about climbing on that windowsill upon hearing Pop's snores to talk to our friends because it was too early to go to bed. She admitted to doing the same thing.

The house had been remodeled to include an indoor bathroom near the laundry room. The kitchen presently served as the master bedroom. Observing an oxygen tank and other paraphernalia of the miner's disease that we all recognized a little too well, I respectfully closed the door.

Our final stop was a private tour of the *Historical Mine Museum of Fenain*. Entering through the front door was like stepping into our home in the *coron* preserved in the style of a coal miner's home of the early 1960s. The coal stove required a double take, it was almost identical to the one in our kitchen on *Rue Taffin*. The oven doors brought back memories of singed hair while trying to dry it in the winter. Walking past an old radio was a flashback of Elisa doing the twist to the music in the middle of our kitchen. On the second floor, we found our ancient school bench, ink well and all. Together with Nadine and Danila, we squeezed in it together, transforming into little giggling school girls.

The last exhibit, fittingly set in the basement, evoked a powerful moment that returned that same sick feeling at the pit of my stomach upon seeing the black mountain for the first time so many years ago. It was a striking image of a coal gallery when the mine still hired children. The miniature replica included a cage in which the miners descended daily to the depths of the earth and then re-ascended at the end of their shift. Beside the cage stood a young child of roughly thirteen years completely covered in soot.

An intense feeling of sadness enthralled me as I thought about Pop, his companions and all of the people who descended in that cage to the pit of the earth in those inhumane conditions. The tears were difficult to keep at bay recalling Pop's desire to sit near a window or why he cultivated the small vegetable garden. It was his little haven, a corner under the blue sky that he had missed so much while he was deep underground.

In that moment, Mr. Dionet placed a precious nugget in my hand, a huge block of coal from the mine *Agache*. Embracing it with care, my heart said, *Thank you Pop, for your sacrifices and I am sorry that this was what you needed to do to save us.*

Our visit in *Fenain* ended where it started, the Town Hall directly across the street. Nadine caught up with Mr. Lebon, her former English professor from high school and Mr. Desobry who taught her sister Annick. They reminisced about their end of school year celebrations that Nadine aided with back in the day by manning the ice cream stand, preparing for school dances and the parade of the floral bicycles.

Through exchanges here and there, I learned that it was through the meticulous efforts of Daniel Dezobry of the *Historic Society of Fenain*, who delved into tons of school records in archives that was instrumental in finding Danila and Nadine. The retired teacher had visited my friends' parents to inform them of the secret plan to track them down for a reunion in March. Nadine spoke as I listened attentively. She said that the news had come to her in surprising disbelief and that there was no doubt that she remembered perfectly well her little friend who had left for America so long ago. One of her fondest memories was the dinner at our home a few days before we departed. It was the first time she had eaten a salad with a vinaigrette dressing that my sister had prepared. I was deeply touched when Danila shared that she thought of me each time she used the china set that they had purchased from us before our departure to America in 1966. Both had articulated that they would not miss this reunion on March 26th for anything in the world.

In closing this uniquely special day, Guy Dionet tapped my shoulder again and smiled. "We are not done yet." I couldn't imagine what could possibly make this already incredible journey any better. Then, an avalanche of books were added to my collection: *Memories through Pictures* by Michel Boulet and *Observing another Time* by Jean-Claude Lebon. Then, Mr. Dionet presented me with *Fenain: La fosse Agache: Le Centenaire de son exploitation 1913 – 2013*, that he co-authored with Renaud Dionet. Everything and more about the coal mine where Pop had worked. A quick flip past the cover took me back to the boy covered in soot earlier in the day. It revealed that the book was dedicated to his father, who had begun his job in the mine at the age of thirteen.

That day, I better understood why Pop had always been so proud to be part of that community. In that instant, my only wish had been to look into Pop's eyes as he faced this beyond heartwarming homecoming.

Overcome with intense emotion, my silence was my mark of respect. That exceptional day was attributed to a surmountable amount of work by many people: from finding my childhood friends, to the elected officials and to all the people of "home." The profound passion of the people of *Hornaing* and *Fenain* around "their" mine inspired a new and better appreciation of the people of the Nord, the mine and the impact on our families that connected us all forever.

In truth, wanting to honor Pop as well as reliving some of my childhood moments turned into a much deeper experience. It gave me a better appreciation for why my parents found it hard to leave their family of the Nord. The kindness and generosity of so many who had made this dream possible for me was

162

priceless. The memories made that day were treasures to guard forever in my heart.

We all agreed that our time together was short as we exchanged contact information and promised to keep in touch. On that day, we not only reconnected with old friends but we made new ones. Unbeknownst of these events, Nadine and her husband had a trip planned to America in May so we would see them again on their tour in Washington, D.C.

It was late and we were all exhausted. We stopped in *Lille* for a very late dinner before boarding the TVG train back to Paris. Still submerged by all of the emotion of the day, I simply wanted to close my eyes and carefully tuck away those memories to replay again and again in my head.

I thought about the lives of my childhood friends…My young friends Danila and Nadine...

Danila was an only child cherished by her entire family. Her almost ninety year old mother had typical aging health problems. Her father died at the end of 2019. He had begun to work at the age of fourteen at the mine of Lemay in *Pecquenourt* just like his father, grandfather, uncles and brothers back in the days when horses still descended the mines. In his early years in the mine, he led horses that pulled the carts full of coal that were ready to ascend. Later, he drove diesel locomotives that replaced the horses. At age twenty-eight, he transferred to the mine of *Agache* in *Fenain*. In 1951, several years after he and Mrs. Huart married, Danila's father, grandfather and uncle built their huge, gorgeous home on the fringes of our *coron*. The home was surrounded by equally beautiful gardens all around the property.

Over time, he honored his promise to his dying father to work outside of the mine in the pure air. His father had died of silicosis at the age of fifty. In 1962, Mr. Huart left the mine to work for the city of *Fenain* until his retirement twenty years later. He remained in relatively good health despite his silicosis that was not recognized as a mine disease since he equally suffered from asthma.

Danila graduated from high school in *Somain* then obtained a diploma in accounting. A few years later she married Philippe and happily settled in *Fenain* where they had two children, a boy and a girl: Cedric and Astrid. Her husband worked for the railroad station, *Society of National Chemin de Fer* (SNCF). Danila worked as an accounting assistant in a brewery for thirteen years. With the arrival of the two children, she was engaged as a teacher's aide for almost twenty years which also gave her the opportunity to spend more time with her children as they grew. In the summer time, they enjoyed the beaches of the Nord, the beautiful Pyrenees and the Alps.

As the children grew older, she took on jobs to care for the elderly while caring for her own aging parents. Additionally, Danila cared for the love of her life, Philippe, who suffered a major heart attack at a very young age and battled cancer. Sadly, Danila lost Philippe not long after the reunion in *Fenain*. Her dear and very close family, as always, was there to comfort her.

Not much changed from the Danila that I remembered of long ago who always cared for others while always having a great outlook on life. She loved her family and what warmed her heart the most was having everyone sitting around the table over a great meal, talking and laughing.

My friend Nadine had a little brother, Gilles, and a little sister Annick born shortly after we separated. Upon finishing high school in *Somain*, she went to nursing school in *Douai*. She graduated in 1980 with plans to work in the medical system of the mine, a model career for many. But the timing was of great concern as the mines were beginning to close all around the Nord. After consulting with the physician who was caring for her father's silicosis, he advised her to pursue a career in the public sector hospital system. Upon graduation, she accepted her first position in a hospital in *Denain* in 1980.

Nadine married Francis whom she met at a school dance while in nursing school. He too was in *Douai* studying Mechanical Engineering at the *School of Superior of the Mines*. They decided to marry while Francis was in the military because their life became more complicated as a young couple in love living far apart while both had very strict parents. Although they tried to be creative in carving time to be with one another, their parents spoke to one another. His parents lived in *Creusot* and expected Francis to visit biweekly. On Nadine's side, being a young girl required her to justify all her dates which were often cut short by early curfews.

The closing of the mines changed their life plans. Francis had plans to work in the mine system because the benefits as an engineer were very attractive with a comfortable house, coal…but that prospect never came to fruition.

Above all, Francis also needed to complete his military service. His first job was near *Maubeuge*. At the same time, they chose to have their children soon after they married: Emilie was born in 1982 and Caroline in 1986. Nadine left her job to raise the children, but she soon found herself missing the work so she returned part time. The company where Francis was employed faced financial hardships and Francis moved to another job in *Beautor*. The two hour commute was hard on the family so Nadine transferred to their hospital center nearby.

Meanwhile, Nadine continued to advance in her professional career. By 1994, a major transformation at the hospital where she worked provided for more challenging opportunities which prompted her to pursue various certifications for health services. As part of the first team to be certified, she was well positioned to work with the director of the hospital. By 2010, she was offered a director position in the retirement home close to her community.

As for Nadine's parents, the closing of the mine of *Agache* in 1976 severely impacted their family. For some time, the workers of the mine of *Agache* were transported to other mines that remained open for some additional time. They worried about where he would be assigned as it quickly became apparent that the care of the personnel or the family needs of the workers were no longer a priority for the mine company. For Mr. Bouriez, he was relieved to learn he was going to the mine in *Arenberg* which was not too far from home. Although the company provided a shuttle for all the workers, Mr. Bouriez drove himself so he could be more independent.

His work ended in 1980 when that mine closed its doors. The family became concerned as Mr. Bouriez was so close to retirement and still had two children in school. He asked to work a few more years after retirement but the offer was denied. He did not take the news too hard because he was already very tired and continued to suffer with silicosis. Nonetheless, Mr. Bouriez was not one to remain idle so he stayed busy doing yard work or do-it yourself projects to earn enough to supplement the family needs.

In 2004, Mr. Bouriez suffered a major heart attack from which he slowly recovered. His last two years of life were the most difficult as respiratory problems aggravated the silicosis along with other health issues. He celebrated his seventieth birthday just before his death in March 2013.

Nadine and Francis settled in their forever home in *Charmes*. Between work, family and their adorable grandchildren, they stayed very busy. Their international travel opened their eyes to other places and cultures, and they developed a real pleasure for discovering other ways of life across other parts of the world. An emotional moment for their family was the return to the native land of her maternal grandparents in a small village of Sardinia in 2012. Above all, they are loyal friends, a strong value they hold close to their hearts. Stemming from Nadine's childhood dream to go to the mountains, they have taken a ski trip each year in the last decade. She and Francis made several weekend trips each year to castles around France. The cities and regions showed a different France than the one imagined from the books of our early years in school. Their ballroom dancing had taken them to the villages of Zagreb in Croatia with other groups who shared the same love of ballroom dance.

My school friends Nadine and Danila were both very close to their families, values that they passed on to their children. The three of us were connected by a past ingrained in our hearts. Between us, we had pursued three different destinies but what was abundantly clear, was that the important things in our lives were not so different. Regardless of our path, we all had the same goal in life, making a better life for our children just like our parents and those before them.

The three of us were of the same mindset that our reunion of March 26th was magical and could not end there. It was up to us to rekindle the light in our futures. In that spirit, a few days later Nadine and Francis met us in Paris on an early Sunday morning for a tour of Versailles on what felt like the windiest day of the year. The photos our husbands captured in front of the castle's golden gates bear witness to the burst of happiness of that day.

We caught up on a half century of life while walking down quaint streets. We warmed up at a bistro with our *old new* friends, in royalty over a champagne lunch. One would never have guessed that we had separated almost a half century ago by the seamless talks and connections. We talked about their visit in America and made plans to see one another soon. Even after a long silence between us, we had renewed the indestructible bond that united us so long ago. In a world of electronic communication, we had freed ourselves of the distance that separated us and quickly linked our past and present. Our goodbye felt like "See you soon."

Our last night in Paris was celebrated at *Au pied du Cochon* situated in *Les Halles* which Jacques had planned forever ago. John and I were delighted that Jacques brought us to this historical place that had such special significance to him. Over dinner we chatted with Simone and Jacqueline, Jacques' wife. We browsed through a folder Jacques had brought with a collection of artifacts from March 26. Included was an article published in *La Voix du Nord:* "Olga, American and daughter of a miner, retraces the steps of her childhood in *Hornaing* and *Fenain*," along with all the highlights of that day. It was proof that it was not a dream…it really happened!

Our long flight home after a few days in Iceland was a time of reflection. Looking at the horizon, John and I pondered about that phenomenal day in the Nord, a fairytale that had all been put in motion by the connection to *Memoire of a Child of the Nord: Hornaing 1950 – 1960.*

I was so proud to share a part of my childhood that had contributed so much to who I had become today, with my husband. If there was any regret, it was only that I could not share that unforgettable journey with our children or my sister. I had expressed to John, who was equally overcome by that experience, my deep appreciation for sharing an incredible journey with me.

The emotions were so profoundly intense, my heart told me that there was something more to do. The fairytale could not simply end there...

Acknowledgments

A profound thank you to Pop, a loving father who has left us far too soon succumbing to Silicosis. It is because of his difficult choices that we, his children, have been able to pave a better future for ours. By extrapolation, it is also a tribute to all of the migrants of the world who, still today, make difficult sacrifices for their loved ones in the hope for an opportunity for a better future.

Thank you to my mother for all of the marvelous days of sitting by my side talking about a life of long ago in our native village to ensure the accuracy of the anecdotes retold. Even in her nineties, the level of detail still vivid in her memory is simply incredible.

Thank you to my siblings, Lisa, Alfredo and Gino for their support and for the countless conversations to fill in the gaps that make our little stories of yesteryear come to life. They pass along a little bit of our yesterdays to the tomorrows of the generations that follow.

Thank you to my husband, John for his patience and unwavering support for my endeavors throughout our years together. Also a huge thank you for the many meals he has prepared so I could finish tying up just one more thought. Thank you to my children, Danielle and Joel, for listening (over and over) to these and many more of my stories over the years. Don't think that it's over …

Thank you to the people in France who have contributed in making my return fifty years later a true fairytale. I owe a wealth of gratitude for that exceptional journey to an immense group of people for their research, to my young school friends, to the elected officials of Hornaing and Fenain, and to the people from "home." Best expressed in one of Enrico Macias' songs, *the people of the Nord have in their hearts the sun that they do not have outside…* That sun is still shining, even a half century later.

Thank you to Danielle Hofmeister, Diwona Kyles, Rogena Kyles and Simone Hérault for all of the time that they didn't have to conduct the many reviews over the course of this writing.

And finally, a special thank you to French author Jacques Pagniez, my Parisian friend and confidante who has faithfully believed in me and my project. Beyond his encouragement, he has stayed by my side from the very first day. He has been an inspiration and an engine for me. After writing Migrant Journey and translating it into French, he devoted an unsurmountable amount of time to help finalize it. That work was published in April 2021 by La Voix Editions under the title *Le Nord, Mon Amérique à moi*. Thank you to Jacqueline, Jacque's wife, for her patience while he devoted countless hours to this project.

About the author

Olga Russo Waters was born in 1957 in Orsara di Puglia, a tiny village in Southern Italy. In 1959, she migrated along with her family to Northern France where her father had found work in the coal mines. In 1966 they migrated to the United States where a part of their family had already settled.

For several decades, Olga held various positions from software code analyst to management roles. Her work was primarily as a contractor in the private sector of civil aviation programs.

Olga and her husband have two children. Now retired, she gardens, reads, takes long walks and plays with her grandchildren.

After writing *Migrant Journey*, she translated the work into French. That work was published by La Voix Editions under the title of *Le Nord, Mon Amérique à moi*, in France.

www.ingramcontent.com/pod-product-compliance
Lightning Source LLC
Chambersburg PA
CBHW020249130626
46549CB00005B/2135